Let's Get Weird

An Anthology of 32 Short Plays & Sketches

By Colin Waitt

Introduction by Kristin McCarthy Parker

LET'S GET WEIRD: AN ANTHOLOGY OF 32 SHORT PLAYS & SKETCHES
© Copyright 2021 by Colin Waitt

ISBN:
978-0-578-92414-4

Editing and layout by Sarah Reynolds
Cover design by Liz Mayer

Contents

Sketches

Introduction
By Kristin McCarthy Parker

One of my favorite things about Colin Waitt, my friend and collaborator, is his ability to laugh at the absurdity of life.

Years ago, while working together on a project in Florida, our daily commute took us past a swamp. It was surrounded by signs reading "Beware of alligators." And positioned perfectly at the water's edge…was a park bench. It tickled us every day, imagining how easy it would be for the gators to make a meal of anyone sitting there.

Then, one day, a person *was* sitting there, happily reading a book. (Our colleagues promised us the bench was safe, and we trusted the locals when it came to gator safety). Still, we couldn't stop laughing at the absurdity of it all. Did the reader find the peace and quietude they were looking for on the brink of death? What book were they reading anyway? While there is no play in this collection about that person, the bench itself does make an appearance. It's Colin's sense of humor to a tee.

I have been lucky to work with Colin countless times over the years, including on his radio play, *From Cold Lake*; his musical, *Little* and *Puffs, Or: Seven Increasingly Eventful Years at a Certain School of Magic and Magic*, which he produced. Whether we're creating together in a sweaty downtown black box, a barn in Maine or Off-Broadway, Colin's steady creative hand makes him a natural center of gravity in the process.

His ability to laugh at the darkness comes in part from his rural Minnesota upbringing. In particular, Midwesterners' polite insistence that everything is *just fine*, even and especially when everything is not. An undercurrent of repressed emotion hums through this collection, such as Pam hinting at her extramarital affair through the metaphor of crop rotation (*Snake Balls in Your Basement*). Sometimes, one must plant soybeans instead of corn to nurture the soil. It is an absurd comparison, but also a bit heartbreaking and totally sincere. Pam, like so many of us, has to muddle her way through the big questions in life with a pitifully small toolbox.

Colin also knows that life's most profound moments don't happen in big, sweeping gestures. They happen in the unplanned, awkward moments in between. Like the two peacocking bros in *Tunnel of Love* who find a glimmer of authenticity on the kitschiest ride at the fair. Even Colin's more playful fantasies, such as William Shakespeare and Anne Hathaway videoconferencing in *King F***ing Lear*, have a lived-in messiness to them that is hilarious and relatable. We make fools of ourselves regularly. We don't keep our cool. In a couple places, this behavior becomes grotesque: characters are pushed over the brink and resort to violence. These pieces, too, are wickedly fun. But overall, Colin is optimistic about our ability to struggle through this mess, however unglamourous.

Through his unpretentious honesty about our silly little lives, Colin has given us this authentic, funny collection. It is an excellent resource for anyone developing and honing their comedic chops. I can't wait to read it on an absurdly dangerous bench somewhere and laugh the whole way through.

Kristin McCarthy Parker is a New York-based director of stage and film. They are the co-founder/director of the critically acclaimed comedy group Recent Cutbacks and directed the stage and film versions of Puffs: Or, Seven Increasingly Eventful Years at a Certain School of Magic and Magic. *www.kristinmccarthyparker.com*

Preface

I love short plays. I wish they'd get their due. I suppose the problem is that, like their fellow ugly stepsisters known as short stories and short films, their primary audience is the people who make them. Short play nights, in New York at least, can have the feel of networking events where emerging professionals hawk their wares. I don't judge (how can one's wares be discovered if they are not first hawked?), but I do wish it felt less like short plays were perceived to be useful only inasmuch as they are a steppingstone to having one's full-length work get noticed. Some of the most surprising, thrilling things I've seen on stage were short plays. When they work, it's heaven on earth.

Maybe that's because it's hard to write a short play. It's hard to tell a full story that doesn't feel undercooked or like a sketch that's outstayed its welcome. And once you've actually written the damn thing, it's hard to rehearse for five, maybe six hours total before putting it in front of an audience. And it's really hard to find *it*, *it* being that magical alchemy when all of the elements and timing come together and the production shines. That's probably because oftentimes a short play's first full run with technical elements and the full creative team present is also the first time it's performed in front of an audience (and sometimes the only time). Maybe that's why watching a great short play is such a revelation: it's a minor miracle it happened in the first place. When it is pushed from the nest, and *it* suddenly takes flight...it's sublime.

I suppose one of the reasons I love short plays is because I've written so many of them. It feels like most playwrights in New York City have a folder on their computer of their full-length plays and a second folder with about ten thousand short plays in it. I am no exception. My short play folder runneth over, and it felt like the right time to let some of them have a life outside of my hard drive.

The works in this anthology are a mixture of things I wrote for short play nights, adaptations taken from longer works, sketches from classes taken at the Upright Citizens Brigade and a few new things written specifically for this book. Maybe you're looking for materials to include in a short play night of your own. Maybe you'll find them useful for a class or speech tournament. Or maybe you're the head of commissioning at Netflix looking for ideas to develop into three seasons of a TV series. In which case, hi (and, sure!). Enough of them are set in Minnesota that it feels worth acknowledging that is where I'm from. Otherwise, you may get to the end and think, "What an oddly specific location to obsess over." It's also worth mentioning they're set there because I love the comic potential of Midwestern passive aggression, its culture of conflict avoidance and the glory of a rural Minnesotan accent. These plays are in no way autobiographical or a comment on any people in my life.

The best part of putting this book together was remembering all of the wonderful people who worked with me to make these plays happen. Few things can compare to the exhilaration of watching the original casts of *Tunnel of Love* and *We Love Work* make magic at *Rule of 7 x7* at The Tank. Or to hear the audience scream with laughter at the first readings of *Hot Dog Eat Dog* and *The Miracle of Birth*. Or in April 2020 rehearsing *King F**king Lear* on Zoom and feeling grateful for the respite from the ambulance sirens that blared 24 hours a day. I have never met so many extraordinarily talented artists as I have living in New York City. But, because the industry is so saturated and there are truly so few opportunities to go around, the majority of us are not working professionally as artists most of the time. What a gift doing these short plays was. For one, maybe two nights only— in spite of the hustle, the juggling, the exhaustion—we got to put on a show. Sure, sometimes it felt duct taped together (or in the case of the plays taken from *From Cold Lake*, there were often more people on stage than in the audience). But, for that brief moment I got to watch those talented people I admire do what they should be doing all the time. Some days the city is a meat grinder, and its competitive edge makes you feel like you'll never be enough. But for ten-ish minutes we were. We were enough. May we all always be enough.

* * *

Writing a play feels like leaping from a plane without knowing if there's a parachute on your back. The works in this book are the ones that survived the drop. There are too many people to thank in this small space, but here are some folks I feel it's important to highlight:

All of the producers, directors and casts of the original readings and productions.

Past and present members of my weekly writing group, including A.J. Ditty, Cat Crawley, Brandon Duncan, Jack Gilbert, Joanna Gurin, Gianfranco Lentini, Austin Ruffer, Lilli Stein and Jordan Stovall.

Particular, emphatic thanks is owed to Kyra Bromberg, Mark-Eugene Garcia, Malena Pennycook and Jenna Scherer who gave supportive, critical feedback on pretty much every single play in this book.

Brett Epstein, producer of *Rule of 7 x7* at The Tank, which presented the original productions of *Daddies*, *King F**king Lear*, *Pilot Light*, *Tunnel of Love* and *We Love Work*.

Meghan Finn and Rosalind Grush at The Tank; Stephen Stout at The Peoples Improv Theater; Meredith Burns, Courtney Little and Alex Tobey at Art House Productions and Erin Mee at This Is Not a Theater Company. They provided innumerable opportunities for me to develop as a writer.

Sarah Reynolds for patiently editing and laying out this book and Tilted Windmills Theatricals for giving the two of us the opportunity to learn how to self-publish the script for *Puffs*.

Liz Mayer for her incredible cover and Xan Weiser for introducing us.

Special thanks is due to the people who gave sketch-specific feedback. Namely, my teachers at UCB—Marshall Stratton and Stephanie Bencin— as well as Ian Gregory Hill, Nate Huntley and Christine Lawless.

The actors who read the final drafts of these scripts over Zoom: Jessie Cannizzaro, Nick Carillo, Anna Dart, A.J. Ditty, Alex Haynes, Sonia Mena, Eleanor Philips and Courtney Roche.

And finally, the biggest thank yous are for my dad, Chris Waitt, and my husband, Harry Waller.

The night before I moved to New York, my dad told me he hoped I could take the weird things I've lived through and write them into something special. I'm not able to comment on the quality of this anthology, but I hope it makes him proud.

Harry has been my cheerleader and champion through life's highs and very, very lows. He is funny, kind and ludicrously talented. I hope one day some of that will rub off on me.

This book is dedicated to the two of them.

Notes on the Text

A slash (/) indicates the next character's line begins and overlaps.

Words in [brackets] should not be spoken but are implied. I often find actors have a bit of anxiety about this, and they wonder if they should actually say the bracketed words. Nope! For example, "I should [go]" would be spoken as "I should."

An ellipsis (…) in place of a character line is an active beat. Depending on the context, it could be a moment of thinking, assessing, deciding, avoiding, panicking, challenging, etc.

The best performances I've seen of any of these plays succeeded because the actors played the characters like they were real people. Sure, a lot of these roles feel particularly weird on the page...but then a lot of real people are weird in their own particular ways. Most of us, actually. Go ahead and lean into the silly, but keep the performances grounded enough that you wouldn't be surprised to see these characters at the grocery store, on the train or in the mirror.

PLAYS

Here on a Sunday

WHERE
The mayor's office in the very, very, very, very, very small town of Cold Lake, Minnesota.

WHEN
Spring 1996, evening. The snow has melted, and change is in the air.

CHARACTERS
PAM – 30s/40s. Administrator at City Hall. Traditional in her thinking. Deeply uncomfortable in her own skin and doesn't think much of herself. Quietly romantic.

MIKE – 30s/40s. Mayor of Cold Lake. Feels like an outsider even though he's lived here his whole life. Also quietly romantic.

A NOTE ON THE TEXT
This play is set in rural Minnesota, and as such it's helpful if the characters speak with thick working-class MN accents reminiscent of *Fargo* or *Drop Dead Gorgeous*.

PREMIERE
Here on a Sunday was originally performed as part of *From Cold Lake: Episode 1*, which received its world premiere at The Peoples Improv Theater (Ali Reza Farahnakian, Founder and Caretaker; Stephen Stout, Artistic Director) in New York City on August 8th, 2016. The producers were Matt Cox, Kristin McCarthy Parker and Stephen Stout. It was directed by Colin Waitt. Songs and Score were composed by Tommy Crawford. Sound design & mixing was by Matt Cox. The cast was as follows:

PAM: Courtney Roche
MIKE: Colin Waitt

The mayor's office. A couple of flags. Photos of Mayor Mike Mueller at community events and in front of city hall.

Mike sits at his desk, distraught.

Keys jangle in the door. Pam enters, flustered.

These first lines should overlap and happen quickly. Think: chickens clucking at one another but not really listening to what the other says.

PAM: Oh, the lights are on. Hello?

MIKE: That you, Pam?

PAM: Mayor Mueller?

MIKE: It's me.

PAM: I thought it might be.

MIKE: Hi.

PAM: 'Cause of your voice.

MIKE: How ya doin'?

PAM: And your face.

MIKE: Hi.

PAM: I can see your face.

MIKE: Come in, Pam.

PAM: It's me, Pam.

MIKE: I know.

PAM: Just 'cause you had asked before.

MIKE: I did.

BOTH: *(Not in unison)* What're you doing here on a Sunday?

(Tiny pause.)

MIKE: Oh, I came here to. Sorry, you go. No, you go. I was just saying I'm here to. Oh gosh. I'm just gonna sit back, and. Please.

PAM: I needed to. Sorry, you first. I insist. No, you go. I came here 'cause. Haha! After you.

(Tiny, anxious pause.)

5

PAM: Ted and the kids are watching *The Simpsons*. Not my thing. Figured I'd come here and do some work, clear my head.

MIKE: You don't like The Simpsons?

PAM: Nope. *The Simpsons*. *Star Trek*. *Seinfeld*. Don't get 'em, don't like 'em.

MIKE: 'Cause they start with an S?

PAM: *(Nicely)* 'Cause of their general tone and content.

MIKE: But why come here? Take a walk. Make some crafts.

PAM: Not as satisfying as filing everything in alphabetical order, ya know?

MIKE: *(Concerned)* ...What order is it in now?

PAM: Missed you at the bake sale.

MIKE: I'm sure no one noticed.

PAM: I did.

MIKE: ...

PAM: ...

MIKE: ...

PAM: What're you doing here, Mayor?

MIKE: ...

PAM: ...

MIKE: Oh.

PAM: ...

MIKE: Pam. Do people like me?

PAM: Sure they do! You've only been mayor for / eight years.

MIKE: Eight years, yah, but no one's ever run against me.

PAM: 'Cause they know they'd lose.

MIKE: I always thought it was because no one else cared.

PAM: ...

MIKE: ...

PAM: You ok?

MIKE: ...

PAM: ...

MIKE: Vicky and I were going to plant what we call our "For the Neighbors" flowerbed. 'Cause we always say / it's more for them than it is for us.

PAM: It's more for them than it is for us, yah. We have one too.

MIKE: ...

PAM: ...

6

MIKE: We had our cartons of petunias and snap dragons all ready to be transplanted. And we walk over to the bed...and there are all these, well, I can't believe it at first. I have to stare at it a while to make sure it's real. Right there in the flower bed...it's a bunch of minnows.

PAM: ...Can they survive in dirt?

MIKE: No, they don't. They die in dirt. And they had. They were dead. Dead minnows. Someone had arranged them to spell out, "Mike Mueller——." I can't even say it.

PAM: ...

MIKE: "Mike Mueller Sux." With an X.

PAM: *(Shock)* An X?

MIKE: Yah. Vicky said it was fine, that the iron would be good for the plants, But I could tell she was only saying it for the neighbors, 'cause you could see them watching us from their "For the Neighbors" flowerbed that / faces our home, yah.

PAM: Faces your home.

MIKE: I needed to come here to, to reflect.

PAM: ...

MIKE: ...

PAM: ...

MIKE: Do I...sux?

PAM: I think what people do think...sux...is when the local government... You raised their taxes, Mayor.

MIKE: But it's for the school!

PAM: I know, but—

MIKE: Education matters! They spelled sucks with an X!

PAM: Normally that sort of initiative goes on the ballot.

MIKE: Those always get shot down!

PAM: Exactly. No one wants to pay for a cow if their kids don't get the milk or they don't believe in the quality of the beef. Even if the calcium's good for our community's bones. You know what I mean.

MIKE: Maybe.

PAM: I mean, even Ted was. Ted was. Let's just say it wasn't just *The Simpsons* that brought me here, though honestly, I don't like that show.

MIKE: Oh, Pam.

PAM: You know. It can be hard to work for a place that people are just kind of programmed to hate. And I only answer phones and keep track of the calendar. Who am I? But people can be. Ted can be. You did a right thing. There may not be one THE right thing. But you did a right thing, and some people just won't like it. And it sucks. It C-K-S sucks.

(As before, these apologies should overlap like chickens.)

MIKE: I'm sorry it's affecting your—
PAM: No, I'm sorry.
MIKE: Don't be. I'm sorry.
PAM: I'm sorry you're sorry.
MIKE: I'm sorry you're sorry I'm sorry.
PAM: Well, I'm sorry you're sorry I'm—
MIKE: We're both sorry.
PAM: Sorry.
MIKE: Sorry.
PAM: Anyway, you'll be reelected. Don't worry about it.
MIKE: Does it mean anything when no one else tries?
PAM: Yes.
MIKE: I just want to be liked.
PAM: Well, for what it's worth...I...like you.

(The room is suddenly filled with repressed sexual tension.)

MIKE: ...
PAM: ...
MIKE: ...You do?
PAM: I, uh. Mhmm. Uh, I, I do.
MIKE: ...
PAM: ...
MIKE: What else...do you...like?
PAM: Oh. Gosh. Um. I don't, um.
MIKE: ...
PAM: I like apples. And apple flavored candy. Apple juice.
MIKE: Uh-huh.
PAM: I like camping and the smell when it rains. The Olive Garden. Actually, "like" really doesn't—I LOVE the Olive Garden.
MIKE: They've just opened one in St. Cloud.

PAM: I know! It's like we're finally real!

MIKE: It is. It's like we're finally real.

(Romantic Italian music fades in.)

MIKE: What is it you like about the Olive Garden?

PAM: The bread. And the salad dressing. And the feeling that I'm a part of something much bigger than little old me here in little old Cold Lake. When I go there, I could be in any Olive Garden, anywhere on earth. Paris. Florida. Or...or...

MIKE: Or Italy.

PAM: Or I could be in an Olive Garden in Italy.

MIKE: I've never been.

PAM: To the Olive Garden?! You must go. You really must, Mayor. It'll change your life.

MIKE: ...

PAM: ...

MIKE: Maybe one day we could. Go. Together.

PAM: Yah. Maybe.

(They move closer. And closer. And closer. Omigod are they going to kiss? Are they going to kiss??!!

Suddenly, they both pull away. The music stops. They verbally vomit:)

MIKE:	PAM:
How 'bout this weather? No more snow this year. That's for sure. At least until the end of the year when it's winter again. Maybe we should stock up on holiday stuff now. Oh really? Be nice to have some real gorgeous weather.	Oh, it's been real good weather lately. Going to have to wear shorts soon. Supposed to get up to the low eighties in the coming weeks. The almanac says this will be a summer to remember. Yah, really! They're saying expect gorgeous weather.

(A truly awkward pause.)

PAM: I should probably [go].

MIKE: Your head feel clearer?

PAM: ???

9

MIKE: You said you came here to clear your head.

PAM: Oh. Uh. Ya know [no]. Bye, Mayor Mueller.

MIKE: Please. Call me Mike.

PAM: Bye. Mike.

MIKE: ...

PAM: Say, uh, you gonna be around a little longer?

MIKE: Uh. I can be.

PAM: It's just. I suddenly thought it might be fun to drive into town and get something to go from the Olive Garden. You want anything?

MIKE: What would you suggest?

PAM: Everything.

MIKE: What if you had to pick one thing?

PAM: Well, the salad dressing is incredible. You could just drink it. But, for my money, the unlimited breadsticks are just. Wow.

MIKE: Nice.

PAM: Though I don't think you can get unlimited to go.

MIKE: How unfair.

PAM: That's life, I guess.

MIKE: Why don't you surprise me?

PAM: Ok.

MIKE: Just nothing that sux.

PAM: I'll do my best.

MIKE: Hey, Pam?

PAM: Yes...Mike?

MIKE: ...

PAM: ...

MIKE: *(With deep meaning)* I'm glad we got an Olive Garden.

PAM: Me too, Mike. Me too.

(Pam exits.

Mike sits at his desk, quietly hopeful.)

END OF PLAY

King F**king Lear

WHERE

A video call. London. Stratford-Upon-Avon. Maybe this happens on something like Zoom. Maybe this is two actors on stage facing the audience.

WHEN

Late morning, 1606.

CHARACTERS

WILLIAM SHAKESPEARE – Yes, that one. Stressed but creative.
ANNE HATHAWAY – The original one. Hanging on by the last goddamn thread.

A NOTE ON THE TEXT

These characters may be snarky about many things, but when it comes to their love, their fear, their deep loneliness…all of that should be played truthfully. Let the stakes be much higher than they may appear at first glance.

To the Shakespeare aficionados who read this, let's agree that this play about two Elizabethan people interacting online is not meant to be 100% historically accurate. For the next ten minutes, let's focus more on fun than biographic detail. To that end, the characters can speak with English accents or not depending on what feels comfortable for the actors.

PREMIERE

King F**king Lear received its virtual world premiere as part of *Rule of 7 x 7: Social Distance Edition* (Brett Epstein, Producer) at The Tank (Meghan Finn, Artistic Director; Danielle King, Managing Producer) on April 18th, 2020. It was directed by Colin Waitt.

WILLIAM: Harry Waller
ANNE: Eleanor Philips

William and Anne video chat.

ANNE: Can you see me?

WILLIAM: There you are.

ANNE: Hello?

WILLIAM: Oops, my sound was off.

ANNE: William Shakespeare.

WILLIAM: My wonderful wife, Anne. I miss you.

ANNE: I miss you too.

(To something unseen)

Hey! Get out of here! Get!

(To William)

William, we really have to do something about these rats.

WILLIAM: Anne, they're our daughters.

ANNE: That hasn't been proven.

WILLIAM: The births were vivid.

ANNE: *(To unseen daughters)* Girls, hey! Hey! Listen, I want you to be strong, independent women as much as the next person, but now that you're home can't you do some cooking and cleaning and laundry? You drank from my breast; I cleaned poop off your butts. The least you can do is mop. And they're gone. How sharper than a serpent's tooth it is to have a thankless child, ammirite?

WILLIAM: Ooo! That's good. Can I use that in something?

(Anne pours herself a large gin.)

ANNE: Whatever you like. Anyway, that's the update from Stratford-Upon-Avon where I guess dreams go to die. How's London?

WILLIAM: Well, it's London in 1606, so it's a lot of people. All of them filthy. Few with teeth. There's plague in the air and everyone's living each day like it's their last. Because it probably is.

ANNE: Oh, William. I worry about you. Come home.

WILLIAM: My love, I can't travel.

ANNE: Just wear a mask. Bloodletting is also supposed to be effective.

(William sighs sadly.)

No, you're right. You're right. This Bubonic Plague is pretty, uh. You're the wordsmith. You describe it.

WILLIAM: It's pretty fucking bad. Oh golly! I've just coined another phrase.

(Writing)

"Pretty fucking bad."

ANNE: Are you keeping busy?

WILLIAM: Well, I've moved past the initial phase, which was feeling like a sad potato. I slept 'til whenever I woke up, stared at my wall, marveled that people were still bear-baiting—can you believe it?! Bear-baiting when we should be social distancing?! Then I'd drink until I fell asleep.

ANNE: Oh, William.

WILLIAM: But now that we're here in month ten? twelve? I mean, what is life? Since I can't make plays, I was thinking of retraining as a greengrocer. But then I thought: pull yourself together. You're William Fucking Shakespeare. Just write, dammit! Also, picture that article in *The Times* six months after all of this finishes and it's a profile of someone like Thomas fucking Middleton, that shit head. Can't you just picture it? Something about how he wrote some masterpiece while quarantining during the plague. Isn't he brilliant, this Thomas Middleton, author of *The Honest Whore*? Forget that William Shakes-whatever. All hail the man who wrote *The Honest Whore*.

ANNE: *(To an unseen daughter)* Stop right there.

WILLIAM: Sorry?

ANNE: Two seconds, lovely.

(To the unseen daughter)

There are three women living in this house and there is an excess of hair in the shower drain. It's not mine. I don't want to blame anyone. I don't want to point any fingers. But I see you, Susanna. I see you, and I see your hairline. Don't go. I'm not finished. I'm not finished. I need you to go to the liquor store. Here's ten farthings, a half penny, and a testoon. I need you to buy me gin. I don't care which brand. Whatever they have. All of it. If it's too heavy, ask your sister. She has arms, she doesn't have a job. Mama needs gin. Mama needs—and she's gone. Kids. That was a choice.

(Back to William)

Sorry, honey! Unprecedented times. Just coping how we can.

WILLIAM: Anne...are the girls ok?

ANNE: Yes!

WILLIAM: ...Are you ok?

ANNE: William, please come home.

WILLIAM: ...

ANNE: ...

WILLIAM: ...

ANNE: I've interrupted your story. I'm sorry.

WILLIAM: No, it's. It's stupid.

ANNE: Please. Tell me how your insecure jealousy is motivating you to do things.

WILLIAM: I did it. I wrote a new play.

ANNE: That's wonderful!

WILLIAM: It's weird. It's long. It's very long.

ANNE: Most of your plays are long.

WILLIAM: I call it *King Lear: A Comedy*.

ANNE: *King Lear: A Comedy*. Sounds fabulous. What's it about?

WILLIAM: It's super light. Role reversals, metaphorical doors slamming, crazy people.

ANNE: Crazy people are very funny. So, what's the story?

WILLIAM: So, there's this king called Lear, and he's like, "I'm old. I'm crazy. I should probably retire." And he has three daughters: Goneril, Reagan, and Cordelia.

(Anne loses her shit.)

ANNE: What the fuck kind of names are those for kids?!

WILLIAM: So, he's like, "Hey daughters, each of you is going to get part of my kingdom. But first! You gotta tell me how much you love me."

ANNE: Good luck getting your kids to do that! Oh, William, this is the funniest shit you've ever written.

WILLIAM: And Goneril and Reagan give him all this praise and he gives them all this land.

ANNE: But not new names?

WILLIAM: But not new names. Then Cordelia—she's his favorite—she's like, "Oh father, I love you so much there aren't words that do it justice, so I'm not going to say anything. Like, putting it into words would actually diminish the love I have for you."

ANNE: Oh wow.

WILLIAM: I know. The idiot! Ha!

ANNE: No, I mean that's actually quite beautiful.

WILLIAM: We'll have to agree to disagree. And King Lear is like, "Are you fa-reakin' kidding me? You're not going to tell me how much you love me? Girl, you cray. You get nothing! BAHAHAHAHA!"

ANNE: Uh, William, I don't want to be a spoil sport, but, um…is that funny?

WILLIAM: It's dark comedy. Very cerebral. Oh! And we'll probably want to cast one of those actors who's an adult woman but has a child voice. She can be like, "Oh golly, now I've done it!" That'll be her catch phrase. "Oh golly, now I've done it!"

ANNE: I think I'm missing something.

WILLIAM: Well, Shakespeare isn't for everyone.

ANNE: *(Surprise)* AAAAAAAAAAAAAAAAAAH!!!!!!

WILLIAM: What's wrong?

ANNE: It's just Judith.

(To the unseen Judith)

Judith, darling, don't sneak up on me like that. Your face is terrifying.

WILLIAM: She can't help it.

ANNE: *(To Judith)* I know you can't help it, but please don't pop out of the shadows like that. Not with that underbite. Also, what are you still doing here? Didn't you go help your sister at the liquor store? Are you going to say anything? Say something. Say something. Well, nothing will come of nothing.

WILLIAM: *(Writing)* Oooh, that's good. Can I steal that?

ANNE: Ugh, now she's tweeting.

WILLIAM: Tweeting?

ANNE: Yes. She jots down a sassy comment, often with spelling mistakes, and force feeds it to a pigeon who then flies off and shits it on the masses as they go about their day.

(To Judith)

Judith, is this really how you want to be remembered? Tweets? Where are you going? Don't run. Don't—and she's gone.

WILLIAM: Should I be concerned?

ANNE: So, what happens next in your *King Lear: A Comedy?*

WILLIAM: Well, Lear gives his land to Goneril and Reagan and then they treat him really badly. Like, really bad. And Lear is all, "Oops! That was a mistake!" That's his catch phrase.

ANNE: "Oh golly, now I've done it!"

WILLIAM: No, that's Cordelia. "Oops! That was a mistake!"

ANNE: So many catch phrases. So, how does it end?

WILLIAM: So! Lear realizes that Cordelia did indeed love him the most.

ANNE: Aw.

WILLIAM: But they're both sentenced to death.

ANNE: Oh.

WILLIAM: Only he doesn't die.

ANNE: Aw.

WILLIAM: But she does. And he brings her body on stage and howls his signature, "Oops! That was a mistake!" And then he dies. And so does everyone else. And then I picture some sort of quippy madrigal or dueling harpsichords, maybe with puppets? And that's the end of the play.

ANNE: Well. Wow. I don't know what to. Wow.

WILLIAM: Would you profile it in *The Times?*

ANNE: William, those daughters are awful creations. Not only in name.

WILLIAM: Thank you...?

ANNE: Is it weird...they kind of make me grateful for our girls?

WILLIAM: What are you talking about? All you've done is complain about them.

ANNE: I mean, they're driving me crazy, but this King Lear's daughters actually drove him crazy. And you know me. I'm not normally like this. It's. This has been a lot.

WILLIAM: I know.

(Anne pours herself an exceptionally large tea from a pot.)

ANNE: I'm supposed to be the parent, but what am I supposed to tell them? That everything's going to be ok? Well, I don't know. Is it? I feel like I'm in adult drag. I'm a drag adult.

WILLIAM: It's very convincing.

ANNE: It's the hands that give it away because they're holding a teapot that's full of—surprise!—gin.

WILLIAM: Have some water.

ANNE: It's 1606. No one drinks the water. We drink gin. What if someone I love catches this thing? What if I do? I don't want any of us to die alone in some medical examiner's room. We've already lost Hamnet. I can't...I can't lose anyone else. This is like a play. It's like living in a bad play.

WILLIAM: Like *The Honest Whore*.

ANNE: This is exactly like *The Honest Whore*. Please. This isn't the gin talking. I love you. I really love you. And I'm terrified. PLEASE. Come home.

WILLIAM: ...

ANNE: ...

WILLIAM: I will. Someday. Can you imagine? Centuries from now, people will think of a plague as something that happened to strange people in strange clothes in a strange thing called the past. They will have no idea how fragile their world is. But it will be. It will always be so, so fragile.

ANNE: Ah, Christ. It's starting to rain.

WILLIAM: Well, this is England.

ANNE: You know, I have a good feeling about this *King Lear*. Though I think it actually might be a tragedy.

WILLIAM: It's the funniest thing I've written.

ANNE: Well, time will tell. So, feel free to use all my lines, BUT! The proceeds from it should be used to buy me something nice. A new bed maybe.

WILLIAM: I'll gladly buy you a new bed. Or at least give you my second best bed.

ANNE: Second best?

WILLIAM: It's hard to make money as an artist. But you'll get a bed of some kind. I promise. You're my Anne.

ANNE: And you're my Will.

WILLIAM: ...

ANNE: ....

WILLIAM: ...

ANNE: Mr. Shakespeare...the girls aren't around...why don't you slip into my DMs and send me some pictures...of your Richard.

WILLIAM: Which one? The second? The third?

ANNE: Your Richard. Send me some pics of your Rick.

WILLIAM: Pics of my Rick? Oh, I get it.

    (Writing)

    Rick pics. They'll be saying that for years.

ANNE: *(Taking off an item of clothing)* Oh, William!

WILLIAM: *(Likewise taking something off)* Oh, Anne!

ANNE: William!

WILLIAM: Anne!

ANNE: *(To unseen daughters, caught)* Oh God! Girls! It's not what it looks like!

END OF PLAY

Daddies

WHERE

Lucas's apartment in Brooklyn.

WHEN

Tonight.

CHARACTERS

LUCAS – 30s. Direct.
DANIEL – 30s. Not Direct.

PREMIERE

Daddies received its virtual world premiere as part of *Rule of 7 x 7: Socially Distanced PrideFest Edition* (Brett Epstein, Producer) at The Tank (Meghan Finn, Artistic Director; Danielle King, Managing Producer) on June 19th, 2020. It was directed by Colin Waitt.

LUCAS: Matt Bovee
DANIEL: Colin Waitt

Lucas and Daniel in Lucas's apartment.

Daniel is distracted.

LUCAS: [...] And then he laughed at me, this senior at NYU or PACE or wherever, and he was like "Well, you've officially graduated from a Twink to a Daddy." And I was like, "Listen—"

DANIEL: Not to change the subject, but we need to talk.

LUCAS: ...Can I finish my story?

DANIEL: No. Um.

LUCAS: ...

DANIEL: So, do you remember the night we, um? You know...

LUCAS: / Yes.

DANIEL: It was a couple of months ago when everything was starting to fall apart, and we were like "Let's get drinks because the world is burning" so we met in the middle? Was it Greenpoint?

LUCAS: It was Greenpoint.

DANIEL: And we were out for drinks and James's Blunt's "You're Beautiful" was playing and we were like, "Why?"

LUCAS: You don't have to keep describing it; I know what night you're talking about.

DANIEL: And our eyes met, and you touched my hand and suddenly it became romantic even with "You're Beautiful" somehow getting louder and louder the longer it played.

LUCAS: Daniel. You're talking about the night we—

DANIEL: It was the night we /made love.

LUCAS: Fucked.

DANIEL: We made love!

LUCAS: We definitely fucked.

DANIEL: You cried as you looked into my eyes.

LUCAS: Because you were pulling so hard on my beard I felt like my face was going to detach from my body.

DANIEL: I guess we just remember it differently.

LUCAS: I never would have pegged you for someone so—

DANIEL: Never mind.

LUCAS: My nipples have finally scabbed over.

DANIEL: Forget I—

LUCAS: I hope I didn't give you the wrong idea, because I'm not—

DANIEL: No, I know.

LUCAS: Looking for anything serious right now.

DANIEL: Neither am I.

LUCAS: And I really value your friendship.

DANIEL: Totally. We're on the same page.

LUCAS: ...

DANIEL: ...

LUCAS: So, this twink was like, "Now you're a Daddy." And I was like, "Listen. Even though I've never heard of whatever-her-name-is that's apparently your generation's Beyoncé, I am still young and with it and—"

DANIEL: I DON'T KNOW HOW TO SAY THIS. Um.

LUCAS: Are you in love with me?

DANIEL: No.

LUCAS: Did you give me an STD?

DANIEL: No, but *you* gave me *something*. Oh God. How do I say this without making things weird?

LUCAS: ...

DANIEL: I'm pregnant. There's a baby inside my body. I'm pregnant with a baby. It's our baby.

LUCAS: ...What?

DANIEL: I'm pregnant with your baby.

LUCAS: How?

DANIEL: Well, my doctor at the Urgent Care said there is literally no scientific explanation, so he referred me to a gynecologist, which was a weird experience for both her and me. And she did an ultrasound, and this is our baby.

(Daniel pulls out an ultrasound.)

Look: it has your beard.

LUCAS: That's an arm.

DANIEL: Yes, that makes more sense. And as the doctor and I watched this little baby float in the as-yet-unnamed equivalent to a uterus that is I guess inside my body, she turned to me and said, "You know, Daniel, I did my undergrad at Johns Hopkins and went to Harvard Medical School. I have literally never seen anything like this before. This is a miracle."

LUCAS: WHAT THE FUCK?!

DANIEL: I know.

LUCAS: BUT WHAT THE ACTUAL FUCK?!

DANIEL: Surprise.

LUCAS: This is impossible!

DANIEL: Not according to my gynecologist.

LUCAS: Oh my God.

DANIEL: So, we should keep it, right? I'm mean, we're going to keep it.

LUCAS: ...What?

DANIEL: Right?

LUCAS: I mean, WHAT?

DANIEL: Haven't you ever wanted to be a dad?

LUCAS: Yes, but WHAT IS THIS CONVERSATION?!

DANIEL: I want to be a dad too.

LUCAS: I'm broke.

DANIEL: Me too.

LUCAS: I don't know if I'd trust me with a child.

DANIEL: Look: this just kind of happens for a lot of people and it isn't something they plan for.

LUCAS: I mean. I mean. What would we even name it? Edith? Ethel?

DANIEL: Stop saying awful names.

LUCAS: Jebediah? Chuck?

DANIEL: ...So, you're in?

LUCAS: I, I, I, I, I, I, I, I, I...Aren't you scared?

DANIEL: Terrified.

LUCAS: ...Don't take this the wrong way, but...Daniel, I don't. I don't know if I want to have a child with you.

DANIEL: You say that like I'm an unfit person.

LUCAS: You bruised my thighs so badly I've been squat walking for months.

DANIEL: Well, not all of us kiss like we're Julie Andrews in *The Sound of Music.*

LUCAS: ...

DANIEL: Sorry. Look, it's your choice to be involved. It'd be great to do this together, but if you have to walk away...I can respect that. It would be scary, but...I mean, it's already scary, but...I'm going to do this no matter what. I really want to be a dad. I've actually been having this fear that I'll never get financially stable enough to, you know, procure a child when the——

LUCAS: Right.

DANIEL: 'Cause it's not like I can just [have one]——

LUCAS: I know.

DANIEL: I don't want to be ninety by the time I can afford to be a. If I can ever afford to be a. So, this is crazy. But kind of serendipitous. And definitely once-in-a-lifetime, so.

LUCAS: ...

DANIEL: ...

LUCAS: ...

DANIEL: ...

LUCAS: Uh.

DANIEL: ...

LUCAS: Well.

DANIEL: ...

LUCAS: I mean.

DANIEL: ...

LUCAS: ...

DANIEL: ...

LUCAS: ...

DANIEL: ...

LUCAS: Ok.

DANIEL: Yeah?

LUCAS: Do we have to get married?

DANIEL: Of course not. We can just be two friends who made love that one time.

LUCAS: Saying "made love" kind of minimizes the fact that you force-fed me your briefs.

DANIEL: Sorry.

LUCAS: I liked it.

DANIEL: I know.

LUCAS: So, when you give birth is it just going to push out of your penis?

DANIEL: Unclear. Unclear.

LUCAS: Just when you thought the world couldn't get any weirder.

DANIEL: ...

LUCAS: I hope we do right by them, whoever they turn out to be.

DANIEL: Me too.

LUCAS: And I hope they feel loved, our little Mabel or Phyllis.

DANIEL: I'm naming the child.

(Lucas rubs Daniel's belly.)

LUCAS: Hello in there, Sheldon. You are loved.

DANIEL: Finish your story.

LUCAS: Naw. It's stupid.

DANIEL: So, some wise twenty-one-year-old told you you've graduated from a Twink to Daddy?

LUCAS: And he was real condescending about it.

DANIEL: Shocking.

LUCAS: And I said, "Laugh all you want. You may look like you belong in *Newsies* now, but we all become Daddies in the end."

DANIEL: Profound.

LUCAS: Shut up.

DANIEL: Let's be Daddies.

LUCAS: Yeah. Let's be Daddies.

END OF PLAY

We Love Work

WHERE

A meeting room in a trendy, shared workspace in Manhattan. The kind of place where tons of startups are side-by-side in small offices with glass walls and work is branded as fun. In the meeting room: neon lights, succulents, tropical leaf wallpaper, snacks. There's a sign that says, "Work Like No One's Watching," either physically in the space or imagined over the audience.

WHEN

This afternoon.

CHARACTERS

JANELLE – Late 20s/early 30s. The manager. Visionary. Probably self-identifies as fun.

CAM – Late 20s/early 30s. The Associate Sales Rep (actually CEO). Grounded. Probably self-identifies as a realist.

MARA – Late teens/early 20s. The intern. Terrified. Probably self-identifies as driven.

A NOTE ON THE TEXT

I've watched different groups of actors rehearse this, and the question always came up of how much the play's twist should be played before it's revealed. I think it works best if we fully believe the reality presented prior to the reveal. This can be facilitated by Janelle's reactions to Cam's speaking out of turn being more frustrated and annoyed, rather than scared. After all, who hasn't had an infuriating boss?

PREMIERE

We Love Work received its world premiere as part of *Rule of 7 x 7* (Brett Epstein, Producer) at The Tank (Meghan Finn, Artistic Director; Danielle King, Managing Producer) in New York City on September 5th, 2019. It was directed by Rachel Gita Karp. Tech was by Jonathan Cottle.

JANELLE: Mariette Strauss
CAM: Zoë Garcia
MARA: Kate Margalite

Janelle in a conference room telling off an unseen person who's overstayed their reservation. She is dressed like the sort of person whose career ambition is "Influencer."

JANELLE: *(So nice, SMH)* Yeah, sorry to just barge in on you like that but it's 2:01, and our reservation began one minute ago. All good vibes. Bye! Come on in, Cam! You can come in. Don't be nervous. I won't bite.

(To unseen person)

You forgot your papers!

(She throws the papers offstage and closes the door as Cam enters, trepidatious.)

Take a seat wherever you like.

(Cam grabs a chair as far away from Janelle as possible.)

Ok, but you don't have to, like, sit all the way over there. People don't usually—

(Cam sits closer to Janelle.)

Love it! There you go. So, blah, blah, blah, this is your yearly evaluation, blah, blah, blah but really this is super informal and low stakes. Other places are serious and scary, but not us. Live Your Life LLC is fun! The neon sign says it all.

BOTH: *(Reading)* "Work Like No One's Watching."

CAM: But it's the building's sign, right? Not ours?

JANELLE: Yeah, but we rent here. So, it's us too. I'm so rude! You want a snack?

CAM: No thanks.

JANELLE: Have a snack! There are pretzels and granola bars and omigod look at all this chocolate. And! These! These are my contribution.

(She holds up a carrot.)

CAM: Carrots. Cool.

JANELLE: Thank you. Thank you. I really wanted a healthy option, but like an eco-friendly one, because sustainability is really important to me. So, I called and called and called and emailed and emailed building management. And then when I didn't hear back, I went to their offices and banged on their door and banged and banged and banged and finally they heard me out because persistence pays off. Now all of the building's conference rooms are stocked with these cups filled with carrots freshly peeled by our interns.

CAM: Wow.

JANELLE: Yeah. Intern fingers are typically a little smaller. Plus, you're not exploiting some person in the third world.

CAM: Is that why I can never find them?

JANELLE: The carrots? They're right here.

CAM: The interns.

JANELLE: And this: this is the best part. Look in the cup. It's ionized water. Look closer. A little closer. Keep looking. I promise it's there.

CAM: *(Finally seeing it)* Ah.

JANELLE: There you go. When you ionize water, it makes it have, like, an amazing ph. So, when you drink it, you feel amazing, you look amazing, and it makes you, like, way healthy. Like, you drink it, and you get a super clean colon. Like, my colon is so clean. And! It prevents cancer. Consuming ionized water prevents cancer. So, it's, like, in all of these carrot cups to keep them fresh but also to make sure that everyone in this building is healthier and has a better life. Live Your Life LLC may only rent an office here, but these carrots really allow us to give back to our community.

(Janelle fidgets nervously with her hands or a bangle.)

Speaking of ionized water. MARA! WHERE IS THE WATER?! Interns, amiright?

CAM: *(A slight edge)* Is she peeling carrots?

JANELLE: ...

CAM: You wanted to talk about my / performance?

JANELLE: Let's talk about your performance. So, you've been an Associate Sales Rep for a year now.

CAM: Uh-huh.

JANELLE: How do you feel the year has gone?

CAM: Great, I think!

JANELLE: You like working for a badass lady boss?

CAM: Yeah, that's been pretty cool.

JANELLE: And just, like, better, right?

CAM: Women can be bad bosses too.

(Janelle's eye twitches, frustrated.)

Is your eye ok?

JANELLE: Cam, what is it we do here?

CAM: Live Your Life LLC sells paper clips.

JANELLE: No. We / "Free people from the clutter of the world to open them to euphoric bliss."

CAM: "Free people from the clutter of the world to open them to euphoric bliss," yes. But what we literally do is sell paper clips. Luxury paperclips.

JANELLE: Our sales have not been great.

CAM: It is hard to sell luxury paper clips.

JANELLE: Then you need to reframe the way you look at it. People want to treat themselves to nice things.

CAM: Not to be negative, but that's kind of delusional, right?

JANELLE: ...

CAM: Are you ok?

JANELLE: *(Not ok)* I'm great.

CAM: Your whole body looks clenched.

JANELLE: I've put a lot of work into creating this brand, and even more work into creating this culture. There's fun sayings on the walls.

CAM: That's building management, not—

JANELLE: There are ionized carrots. If you embraced it, if you Lived Your Life LLC our sales would go through the roof.

CAM: But—

JANELLE: But if you can't, then maybe the problem is you. And maybe we shouldn't be working together.

CAM: ...Are you firing me?

JANELLE: I think a better question is: is this what you actually want to be doing?

(Cam suddenly becomes very desperate, feral.)

CAM: Please! Oh God! Please! Please, Janelle. Please. Where would I go?

JANELLE: What are you...?

CAM: I only work 80 hours a week to keep this ship from sinking. I can work more.

JANELLE: Uh—

CAM: Should I sleep here? Should I dump my family?

JANELLE: Cam, uh—

CAM: I'm begging you. I'm on my knees, ok? I'm on my knees and I'm holding an ionized carrot and. Please. We're in this together. I'll do whatever you want.

JANELLE: *(Truly confused)* I don't know what to / um.

CAM: I'll participate in the culture. I'll become a promoter of euphoric bliss.

JANELLE: Cam?

CAM: I'll do whatever you say!

JANELLE: I'm sorry, I don't actually know what to, uh.

> *(Cam's energy shifts. She is the boss. She is high status. She is not pleased. Janelle is suddenly the lowest status person maybe ever.)*

CAM: I've seen all I need to see. The role play is over.

JANELLE: *(A mouse)* I'm sorry, I—

CAM: I said the role play is over. The fuck was that? Did you just try to fire me? I'm your fucking boss!

JANELLE: I got nervous.

CAM: Janelle, this was supposed to be a simple Role Play Evaluation.

JANELLE: You made it weirdly personal.

CAM: All I had to do was pretend I was one of the idiots on our payroll, and all you had to do was talk to me like you talk to said idiots when they underperform. Easy.

JANELLE: I'm sorry. Normally I'm better at team evaluations.

CAM: Oh, so this was just an off day?

JANELLE: Yeah.

CAM: So, it's an excuse. Is that what you're saying?

JANELLE: No, sorry. That's not what I [meant]—

CAM: You're giving me an excuse.

JANELLE: Sorry.

CAM: Stop apologizing! It's about as useful as sticking your nipple in a goat's ass. ARGH! Throw one of the fake succulents.

JANELLE: Excuse me?

CAM: Are you going to make me do it, you incurable athlete's foot? Throw it. Throw it. Throw it!

(Janelle throws a fake succulent, which thwomps against a wall.)

And you blame me?

JANELLE: I didn't say that.

CAM: What was the bullshit about "Is this what I want to be doing" and "Maybe we shouldn't be working together?"

JANELLE: You called me delusional.

CAM: We are in the red, Janelle. These dingbats aren't selling enough paper clips to allow me to cover the basic costs of running my business. We don't actually have enough money to pay them, let alone ourselves. And I'm supposed to pretend this is fun? I would rather breast feed a raccoon.

JANELLE: If people enjoy working—

CAM: They won't sink my fucking ship? I hate to break it to you, Mr. DiCaprio, but it's just the two of us floating here on this door.

JANELLE: I'm sorry.

CAM: Enough with the sorrys!

JANELLE: Sorry.

CAM: Janelle.

JANELLE: I'm sorry.

CAM: GAH! I hate you so much! You're like barbed wire in my urethra. ARGGGGGH! Turn over the table. Turn it over!

JANELLE: *(Trying)* It's heavy.

CAM: Then throw that chair. Throw it!

(Janelle throws a chair incompetently.)

If you can get some bimbo of a man to stock carrots in all these offices, then you can motivate our team to fucking sell $20 paper clips. Sell 'em.

JANELLE: / Ok.

CAM: SELL 'EM. Oh, I feel exhausted. You've exhausted me. Mara! MARA! WHERE IS MY IONIZED WATER?!

(Mara immediately scurries in with the water.)

MARA: Sorry, the ionizer was clogged—

CAM: I don't need excuses; I just need water.

(She drinks.)

Oh, my colon feels amazing. Janelle, based on your performance today, I am putting you on probation.

JANELLE: Please.

CAM: You have one month. One month to inspire our team to blow my tits off with their sales, or—and I don't want to seem vindictive or cruel—but so help me God if you don't, you will never work in this city again. Not selling lifestyles, not selling paper clips, not even picking up trash off the streets. I will make sure no one will touch you. You'll die alone in some tunnel, devoured by rats.

(She goes to leave.)

Oh, and Mara?

MARA: *(Terrified but being nice)* How can I help?

CAM: *(So nice)* That water was really good.

MARA: *(Touched)* Thank you.

CAM: No. Thank you.

(Cam leaves, plopping the still pretty full water glass and any other trash she finds into Janelle's hands.)

MARA: *(Peeling a carrot)* She seems kinda stressed, huh?

JANELLE: Mara.

MARA: You know, at first when I realized I'd be here 30 hours a week and only getting paid with a monthly Metro Card I was kind of, I don't know, like bitter? But, the snacks, the wine on tap—

JANELLE: Mara.

MARA: *(Awe)* She likes me.

(Janelle tosses what remains of the water into Mara's face.)

JANELLE: Mara, I'm gonna need you to clean that up.

MARA: But there aren't any towels.

JANELLE: Not my problem.

(Mara looks around, unsure what to do. Finally, she lays on the ground and wipes up the spillage with her work outfit.

Janelle watches, demeaning Mara becoming increasingly difficult for her to bear.)

JANELLE: Wait. You don't have to. Forget the. I'm sorry. I'm just. I'm sorry.

MARA: No need to apologize.

(Darkly)

I'm going to be your boss someday.

(Chipper)

In the meantime, if you need anything else, just let me know.

(Mara exits.

Janelle stands a moment, determined not to let this negatively affect her. But then reality gets the better of her and she lets out a long, <u>silent</u> primal scream. She silently screams and screams until she is on her knees, a silently screaming mess.

Then, she composes herself and begins to reset the room as something like the chorus of Donna Sumer's "She Works Hard for the Money" plays us out. She dances slightly to the beat.)

END OF PLAY

Alternate Ending for Two Actors

I once saw two actors do this play for a scene study class, and they cut the end section because they didn't have a third actor. It worked but was obviously a bit abrupt since Mara plays so heavily into the final moments. So, I thought it would be fun to write an ending that allowed the play to feel complete when performed by a duo.

CAM: GAH! I hate you so much! You're like barbed wire in my urethra. ARGGGGGH! Turn over the table. Turn it over!

JANELLE: *(Trying)* It's heavy.

CAM: Then throw that chair. Throw it!

(Janelle throws a chair incompetently.)

If you can get some bimbo of a man to stock carrots in all these offices, then you can motivate our team to fucking sell $20 paper clips. Sell 'em.

JANELLE: / Ok.

CAM: SELL 'EM. Oh, I feel exhausted. You've exhausted me. Water! Water! I need water!

(Janelle hands her the carrot cup. Janelle tosses the carrots, and Cam slams the water back.)

Oh, my colon feels amazing. Janelle, based on your performance today, I am putting you on probation.

JANELLE: Please.

CAM: You have one month. One month to inspire our team to blow my tits off with their sales, or—and I don't want to seem vindictive or cruel—but so help me God if you don't, you will never work in this city again. Not selling lifestyles, not selling paper clips, not even picking up trash off the streets. I will make sure no one will touch you. You'll die alone in some tunnel, devoured by rats.

(She goes to leave.)

Oh, and Janelle?

JANELLE: Yes, boss?

CAM: Smile.

(Cam leaves, plopping the carrot cup and any other trash she finds into Janelle's hands.

Janelle stands a moment, determined not to let this negatively affect her. But then reality gets the better of her and she lets out a long, <u>silent</u> primal scream. She silently screams and screams until she is on her knees, a silently screaming mess.

Then, she composes herself and begins to reset the room as something like the chorus of Donna Sumer's "She Works Hard for the Money" plays us out. She dances slightly to the beat.)

END OF PLAY

The Pain of Loving You

This is one of the first short plays I ever wrote. It was for a competition, and the prompt was to write something riffing on classic themes inspired by the idea of "Scandal." The play ended up being a finalist and then was a finalist again for a different, unrelated competition. It would be a very long time until I was once again a finalist or selected for anything else, but this early boost of approval gave me the confidence to keep at it.

WHERE
Grace and Jason's affluent home in Central Minnesota.

WHEN
January, today.

CHARACTERS
GRACE – 20s. Mind in a million places. Has a head cold.
JASON – 40s/50s. What one might call a traditionally masculine man.
MAGGIE – 40s/50s. A Minnesotan Medea ready for revenge.

A NOTE ON THE TEXT
This play is set in rural Minnesota, and as such it's helpful if the characters speak with thick working-class MN accents reminiscent of *Fargo* or *Drop Dead Gorgeous*.

Darkness. A kettle begins to hiss. It increases in intensity and volume until it is unbearably loud.

Then:

Lights up. Grace takes the hissing kettle off the stove.

A cast iron skillet nearby.

Unpacked and partially unpacked boxes around the room.

A bouquet of sad looking fresh flowers.

Snow falling outside the window.

Jason looks intently at various white paint swatches.

Grace periodically blows her very red nose.

GRACE: You sure you don't want some?

JASON: Mmm.

GRACE: Quit smoking to be healthier and instantly get sick. Ain't it the way?

JASON: Ain't it the way.

GRACE: *(Reading tea box)* Connie Olsen says this ginger one is supposed to knock it out, but I don't know.

JASON: *(Re: swatches)* Am I stupid or are these all the same?

GRACE: You got, like, ten different colors there.

JASON: They're all white.

GRACE: No. There's bone. Salt. Dust. Now that one, that one's the white. Or is it lace? Gosh, you stare at 'em long enough and / they all look the same.

JASON: They all look the same, yah.

GRACE: Kinda hurts my eyes.

JASON: Mmm.

GRACE: *(Re: tea)* You sure you don't want some?

JASON: Sit still.

GRACE: Connie Olsen says movement is good for getting the sick out.

JASON: Well, if Connie Olsen said so.

GRACE: She knows things.

JASON: Yeah, from peeking over bushes and listening at windows.

GRACE: She's lonely.

JASON: I believe the word is "nosy."

GRACE: She brought us flowers!

JASON: She pretends she's passed out on the bar at the Lodge so she can listen in on people's conversations!

GRACE: I thought she just had a problem.

JASON: She probably does, but still!

GRACE: Well, I for one think it was nice that she was talking <u>to</u> me instead of <u>about</u> me. More than I can say for, you know, the rest of the street.

(He holds her tenderly.)

JASON: Hey, Rudolph: fuck 'em.

GRACE: Jason.

JASON: Fuck 'em.

(A tender moment.)

GRACE: They are ugly flowers.

JASON: Yes.

GRACE: And they'll probably be dead by the time I'm healthy enough to smell 'em again.

JASON: Classic Connie. Nice but not.

(She wet coughs into his face.)

GRACE: Sorry!

(Jason wipes his face with a tea towel.)

JASON: I guess the tea works.

GRACE: Sorry.

JASON: *(Back at the swatches)* So, what do ya think? Mist? Pearl?

GRACE: Ooo, this one's nice! Dander.

(A sharp knock at the door.)

JASON: You expecting anyone?

GRACE: No. You?

JASON: Maybe Connie forgot to plug in her wiretap.

(He opens the door. Maggie stands there in a heavy winter coat, thick gloves and no hat.)

Maggie. Hi.

MAGGIE: Jason.

JASON: ...

MAGGIE: ...

JASON: Jesus, it's colder than hell out there. What are you doing without a hat?

MAGGIE: Can I come in?

JASON: Uh, sure.

(She enters. He closes the door.)

MAGGIE: Grace.

GRACE: Maggie. Hi.

JASON: If you want, I can take your coat.

MAGGIE: No.

JASON: ...

MAGGIE: ...

JASON: ...

MAGGIE: I brought the papers.

JASON: Oh, uh. Grace, would you...

GRACE: Yah, sure. You don't want to be near me anyway.

MAGGIE: No.

GRACE: 'Cause I'm sick.

MAGGIE: Well, it is flu season.

GRACE: Should have got my shot.

MAGGIE: Bang.

GRACE: Well, I should, uh. I'll just. Gosh, it's really coming down out there, huh?

JASON: Why don't you go in the family room, Grace?

GRACE: Great idea. I need to, uh.

JASON: Why don't you unpack?
GRACE: Yah. Perfect. Ok. Yah. Great. Bye.

(After too long of a moment, she exits.)

JASON: ...
MAGGIE: ...
JASON: ...
MAGGIE: ...
JASON: You sure you don't want me to take your coat?
MAGGIE: ...
JASON: ...
MAGGIE: ...
JASON: She wasn't kidding about that snow. We're really gonna get it, apparently.
MAGGIE: ...
JASON: ...
MAGGIE: ...
JASON: ...
MAGGIE: ...
JASON: You, uh, gosh, you uh, brought them papers, I guess.
MAGGIE: I signed 'em, so it's official. We're divorced.
JASON: ...
MAGGIE: ...
JASON: Well. There ya go.

(The record player turns on loudly in the next room. It is something like the album The Trio, by Dolly Parton, Linda Ronstadt, and Emmylou Harris. A song like "The Pain of Loving You" starts. A few phrases play, then:)

Guess she found the record player.
MAGGIE: I'm surprised she knows how to work it.
JASON: She's not twelve.
MAGGIE: No?
JASON: Why in the hell did she pick this stupid album?
MAGGIE: Does she know this was our song?
JASON: No. Our little secret.

MAGGIE: ...

JASON: You want a drink or something?

MAGGIE: Sure.

(He goes to the fridge and produces two bottles of craft beer.)

You drink fancy beer now.

JASON: Is it fancy?

MAGGIE: Fancier than you bought for me.

JASON: ...

MAGGIE: Nice cast iron skillet.

JASON: That's not a fancy thing.

MAGGIE: My mom had one. Don't know where it ended up.

JASON: I'm not showering her with—

MAGGIE: Maybe it was a garage sale.

JASON: We had nice things too.

MAGGIE: It was probably a garage sale.

(A long beat.

Then, the music scratches in the other room.)

JASON: Ohp. Changed her mind.

(Something like Linda Ronstadt's "You're No Good" begins to play.)

MAGGIE: More Linda Ronstadt.

JASON: Sounds like she put on her greatest hits. The first one.

MAGGIE: That's a good one.

JASON: You remember seeing Linda Ronstadt when we took that trip to Arizona?

MAGGIE: I do.

JASON: Life was different before kids.

MAGGIE: ...

JASON: So different.

MAGGIE: ...

JASON: ...

MAGGIE: ...

JASON: How are the boys?

MAGGIE: ...

JASON: I know I've been really shitty, but uh. I'd like to see them.

MAGGIE: ...

JASON: ...

MAGGIE: ...

JASON: I get to see them. We've signed a legal agreement.

MAGGIE: ...

JASON: ...

MAGGIE: They're in the car.

JASON: They've been out there this whole time?

MAGGIE: Mmm.

JASON: Are you serious? It's freezing out there!

(Maggie takes off her gloves, revealing her hands are stained with dried blood.

She unzips her jacket, and her shirt is similarly covered in blood.)

MAGGIE: You think you're so slick.

JASON: What the hell?

MAGGIE: Mr. Slippery.

JASON: What did you do?

MAGGIE: Mr. Slick.

(Maggie swiftly and easily picks up the skillet and bashes it into Jason's head. He falls to the floor.

Jason's body tremors.)

While I've got your ear, Jason, I just want you to know that all of this is your fault. What kind of monster does this to his family? And now my boys are gone, and it'll be like you never existed and It. Is all. Your fault.

(Maggie whacks his head a final time with the skillet, and he dies.

She returns the skillet to the stove and turns the gas knobs on the burners to high. The home begins to fill with gas.

Maggie washes her hands and then drags Jason's body to the basement door. She opens it. She pushes his body down. She closes the door.

She wipes up any blood.

Maggie sits at the kitchen table and finishes her beer for an unbearably long amount of time. The music continues to play in the background.

Suddenly, Grace re-enters the kitchen, oblivious that anything has happened.)

GRACE: Kinda a fun record, huh? Where's Jason?
MAGGIE: He went to buy more beer.
GRACE: Oh.

(Grace has a mini coughing fit.)

Don't worry, I'm fine. Honestly, I'm ok. I never get sick, I just.

(She hacks some more.

Maggie takes out a cigarette and puts it in her mouth. She pulls out a lighter.)

MAGGIE: Ginger tea supposedly knocks it out.
GRACE: I've heard that. Does it give you back your smell too? YOU CAN'T SMOKE IN HERE.

(Maggie looks at Grace sharply and takes the cigarette out of her mouth. She puts it back in the carton, which she sets on the table.)

I mean, I'd make an exception, but. I just quit. Like a week ago.
MAGGIE: ...
GRACE: Look, I hope there's no. I mean, I know there's hard feelings. But I hope one day we can, we can be friends.
MAGGIE: ...
GRACE: You want some coffee or tea?
MAGGIE: I gotta get home and feed the cat.

(Maggie exits.)

GRACE: You must have been real fun to be married to.

(*Grace notices the cigarettes. She stares at them, desperately craving one.*

She grabs the box and pulls one out, considering it.)

What are you doing? You're sick.

(*She brings the cigarette and carton to the garbage, which she opens.*

She's about to throw them away when…she decides not to.

She reaches into the cupboard next to the stove and produces a pack of matches.

With guiltless relief, she puts a cigarette in her mouth. She ignites the match.)

END OF PLAY

Tunnel of Love

The setting for this play is inspired by Ye Old Mill, the tunnel of love at the Minnesota State Fair. It has all the ingredients for romance: dyed water, seating for four and an array of kitschy window installations made of lawn ornaments and wooden cut-outs. It's glorious.

Tunnel of Love ended up becoming part of an anthology play I wrote called *Fair*, which includes two other works from this collection: *The Miracle of Birth* and *Hot Dog Eat Dog*.

WHERE
The Tunnel of Love at a county fair in central Minnesota. It has been around for generations and therefore has a kitschy, old-timey feel. It's somehow both sweet and ridiculous.

WHEN
Today.

CHARACTERS
CHAD 1 – Early 30s. The man-boy Chad. Probably never destined to peak.
CHAD 2 – Early 30s. The sensitive Chad. Peaked at 17.

A NOTE ON THE TEXT
In my playwright dreams, both Chads speak with thick Minnesota accents a la *Fargo* or *Drop Dead Gorgeous*. Alternatively, they could simply sound like bros. If you're feeling particularly adventurous, they could blend both sounds and be very Minnesotan bros.

"Klaver," as in Local Artist Linda Klaver, rhymes with "Waiver."

PREMIERE
Tunnel of Love received its world premiere as part of *Rule of 7 x 7* (Brett Epstein, Producer) at The Tank (Meghan Finn and Rosalind Grush, Co-Artistic Directors) in New York City on April 18th, 2019. It was directed by Alex Tobey. Tech was by Jonathan Cottle.

CHAD 1: Sean McIntyre
CHAD 2: Will Turner

Splash! A boat in a tunnel of love flume ride begins its journey. The tunnel's speaker system plays old-timey polka music that probably was never romantic. We hear it softly for the whole play.

The silhouettes of two dude-bros—Chad 1 and Chad 2—appear. They sit side by side. Chad 1 has a bag of fair food on his lap.

CHAD 1: Frickin' tunnel of love, man.

CHAD 2: Frickin' tunnel of love. And what's with this song, Chad, dude?

CHAD 1: Chad, bro, I don't know. Apparently, they've played the same music in here since, like, our grandparents were kids.

CHAD 2: Was this ever romantic?

CHAD 1: Chad, bro, I bet your grandparents totally boned to this song. Corn dog?

(Chad 1 pulls a corn dog from his bag.)

CHAD 2: Chad, dude, gross. My grandparents are in their 90s. My grandma has a hunchback, and my grandpa has no teeth. I don't wanna think about them boning.

CHAD 1: Nothing more natural than boning, bro. Teeth or no teeth.

(The boat passes a "romantic" art installation. Perhaps we see it, perhaps we only need to hear about it.)

CHAD 2: What is that?

CHAD 1: Famous tunnel of love decorations, bro.

CHAD 2: It looks like a cage full of fake squirrels, just staring at us.

CHAD 1: It is a cage full of fake squirrels, just staring at us. But they're holding tiny hearts. I guess old-timey people thought it was romantic. To be watched. By a cage full of squirrels.

(He offers:)

Meatball? On a stick?

(Chad 1 pulls a meatball on a stick from his bag. Chad 2 declines. Chad 1 munches on it.)

CHAD 2: Why the frick would Brysen and Kelsey make us follow them in here?

CHAD 1: I think they wanted to get rid of their third wheel, and since they didn't have a trunk, they put us in a boat.

CHAD 2: I feel like that time I went to Disney World and was the odd man out on the Little Mermaid ride. I had to sit in a giant pink shell all by myself and reassure all the parents and their little girls that I'm not some creep who rides the frickin' Little Mermaid ride alone.

CHAD 1: You're not alone, bro. You're with me. Speaking of shells...canned clams? On a stick?

(Chad 1 pulls canned clams on sticks from his bag. Maybe they're on toothpicks?)

CHAD 2: I'm good.

(Chad 1 slurps the clams.)

CHAD 1: Was that your trip to Disney with Carissa's family?

CHAD 2: Oh, man. Look at the time.

CHAD 1: Where is Carissa anyway?

CHAD 2: *(Paddling with his hands)* We're gonna miss the tractor pull. Help me paddle.

CHAD 1: Chad, bro. You avoiding my question, bro?

(Chad 2 pretends he doesn't hear Chad 1.)

Chad. Chad. Chad. Chad. Chad. Chad. Chad. Chad. Chad.

CHAD 2: Carissa's not here 'cause her, uh, her mom, uh, well...You know how they put up that new Verizon tower out by Sartell?

CHAD 1: Yeah.

CHAD 2: Well, the frickin' radio frequency waves have, like, messed up the brains of birds that fly by it. I guess a lot of geese have been thinking they have to like fly south for the winter, even though it's July. So, a few days ago this goose lost its mind and decided it was time to head to Florida and must have also lost the ability to perceive depth and just shapes in general and it flew smack dab into Carissa's mom's face.

CHAD 1: Oh man. Goose to the face.

CHAD 2: Total goose to the face.

CHAD 1: Is she alright?

CHAD 2: She'll regain consciousness again. Probably. On the plus side, I've never had better cell service in my life.

CHAD 1: Yeah, mine's been incredible lately. Potato? On a stick?

(He pulls out a raw potato on a stick.)

CHAD 2: Anyway, Carissa's with her mom in the I.C.U and that is why she's not with me today.

(The boat passes another "romantic" installation.)

CHAD 1: Ah, bro, this one's super weird: lawn gnomes. Styled like Precious Moments figurines.

CHAD 2: You don't need to explain, bro. I can see it too.

CHAD 1: I just want to make sure everything is clear.

(Suddenly, Chad 2 begins to cry.

This is the first time Chad 1 has ever seen Chad 2 so vulnerable, and it's a total WTF moment.)

Oh, you're crying.

CHAD 2: Carissa has a wall of Precious Moments figures. Like an actual wall filled with them. Because she says life is full of precious moments.

CHAD 1: *(WTF)* Uh-huh.

CHAD 2: And she said this goose dive-bombing her mom's face has made her think about how precious life actually is. And how short. And she said that we've been dating since, like, we were fourteen and now that we're thirty-two she wants to know what else is out there.

CHAD 1: Oh, dude. I'm sorry.

CHAD 2: What else is out there? I was the captain of pretty much every sports team in high school. Every dude wanted to be me, and every chick wanted to sleep with me. And I have stayed the exact same person for the past fifteen years and literally not grown or changed at all except that my body has significantly aged. What else is out there, Carissa? I'm as good as it gets.

CHAD 1: Oh bro, I know what you mean. I've never been in a relationship for more than a night. I know! Me! I'm fun! I could talk about myself for hours! And do! Plus, I'm a foodie! What's not to love? Protein Powder? On a stick?

(Chad 1 licks his protein powder on a stick, which is just as awful as you'd imagine. Chad 2 also takes a taste.)

CHAD 2: Man, what do women even want?

(A moment as they sit, both sadly pondering this question that they've literally never thought to consider until right now.)

CHAD 1: You know, my aunt—Local Artist Linda Klaver—she has a lot of feelings. And she normally puts them into quilts or, you know, those signs you make out of wood that you paint inspirational sayings on?

CHAD 2: I know the signs.

CHAD 1: Anyway, my aunt—Local Artist Linda Klaver—sometimes she acts.

CHAD 2: Oh yeah, I saw her in that play, *Cinderella*. It was kinda a lot.

CHAD 1: I know, bro. Turns out she has a lot of primal feelings that she needs to let out. But she says that when she acts, it makes her put herself in another person's shoes, and then she learns a little of what it must be like to be them.

CHAD 2: Huh. What a weird concept that I've literally never thought of before. So, like, I have to physically put on a pair of someone else's shoes?

CHAD 1: She said it's a *(mispronouncing)* metaphor.

(Chad 2 looks at him, confused.)

I don't know what that means either, but maybe instead of actually trying on someone's shoes we imagine what it's like to be them?

CHAD 2: Bro, what a unique idea. You're so smart.

CHAD 1: *(Touched)* Thank you.

CHAD 2: So, I'll pretend I'm a woman.

(Chad 2 "becomes" a woman.)

CHAD 1: Ooo, very convincing. What should I call you?

CHAD 2: Chad. I'm not changing my name just 'cause I'm a lady now.

CHAD 1: That's, like, super inspiring, bro.

CHAD 2: What can I say? I'm Chad. I'm just a gal of today. Now, talk to me like you talk to women.

CHAD 1: Ok. Uh. Hey. You look lonely. And you have lovely breasts. Please enjoy this pic of my dick.

CHAD 2: Dude, this is why you've never been in a relationship for longer than a night.

CHAD 1: Well, excuse me. If it's so easy, show me what you say.

CHAD 2: Fine, I will. Hey, interesting lady. What's your name?

CHAD 1: *(As a woman)* Chad.

CHAD 2: Hey Chad, you ever wanted to be with the most popular guy in high school only now he's thirty-two and cries himself to sleep at night?

(Chad 1 recoils—that's a hard no.)

...What?

CHAD 1: Would it be easier if we just said what we'd want a guy to say to us if we were a chick?

CHAD 2: *(With surprising, inspired conviction)* Well, first of all, I'd say don't call me a "chick." Have a little respect.

(They're both taken aback.)

Whoa, that was surprising.

CHAD 1: Very surprising, but ok. I guess I'd say, Chad, I know you're not the smoothest or the second smoothest or even the second to last smoothest, but deep down in there, real deep down, like you gotta really dig, but somewhere down there, like, beyond when you'd naturally think you'd hit the bottom, somewhere you are a nice person.

CHAD 2: You are.

CHAD 1: Thanks.

CHAD 2: And I'd say, Chad, it can be lonely being a person who is more likely to, I don't know, wash his bathroom towel more than once each season than be an amazing person ever again. But in spite of that, you are capable of becoming a better person. And you are worthy of love.

CHAD 1: Ah, bro. That's beautiful.

CHAD 2: Thanks.

CHAD 1: And you are worthy of love. I love you, bro.

CHAD 2: Yeah?

CHAD 1: Yeah.

CHAD 2: Cool man. I love you too.

(They look at each other and something profoundly changes...Love?

Suddenly, they are both deeply uncomfortable, even nervous.)

CHAD 1: This is gonna sound kinda gay, but is it me or did things just get kinda gay?

CHAD 2: Why are you looking at me like that?

CHAD 1: I don't know. Why are you looking at me like that?

CHAD 2: I don't know.

CHAD 1: Let's look away on the count of three.

CHAD 2: Ok, yeah.

BOTH: One. Two. Three.

(Neither has looked away.)

CHAD 1: Ok, so we're still looking at each other.

CHAD 2: ...Yup.

(Suddenly, they begin to lean in toward each other to kiss. Neither seems to be in control of his own body, though each of their bodies very clearly want to be doing this.)

CHAD 1: You know, sometimes my aunt—Local Artist Linda Klaver—she says that when she's on stage sometimes she gives in to the moment and her brain can't stop her body from doing what it wants to do.

CHAD 2: Like when she starred in *Noises Off* and cried the whole time.

CHAD 1: Or when she was Annie in *Annie* / and just cried the whole time, yah.

CHAD 2: And just cried the whole time. Is that what's happening now?

CHAD 1: No clue. Where's Aunt Linda when you need her?

(The move closer and closer to kissing, calling out for Linda's help as they do.

These lines can overlap.)

CHAD 2: Linda?!
CHAD 1: Linda?!
CHAD 2: Linda?!
CHAD 1: Linda?!
CHAD 2: Linda?!
CHAD 1: Linda?!

(Suddenly, they kiss. It is surprising, passionate, and glorious.

Then panic as each slides as far as possible from the other, neither making eye contact.

Then each tentatively looks toward the other to see if he's looking over, and when their eyes meet, they both look away.

After a moment, they impulsively reach back in and kiss.

They look back out as the boat passes another "romantic" installation.)

CHAD 2: Oh look: a bunch of corn husk dolls / on a Ferris wheel.
CHAD 1: On a Ferris wheel, yah. And it moves. Kinda.

(They both jump, startled.)

BOTH: Ah!
CHAD 2: I guess the dolls move too.
CHAD 1: ...
CHAD 2: ...
CHAD 1: ...
CHAD 2: What just happened?
CHAD 1: I don't know.
CHAD 2: It was—it was weird, right?
CHAD 1: Totally weird.
CHAD 2: I mean, I'm not [gay].
CHAD 1: Neither am I. But.
CHAD 2: What?
CHAD 1: Nothing.

CHAD 2: What, dude?
CHAD 1: I. Kinda. Never mind.
CHAD 2: What the hell you trying to say, bro?
CHAD 1: I kinda. Maybe. Didn't think it was. Bad.
CHAD 2: ...
CHAD 1: Sorry. Forget I.
CHAD 2: I didn't think it was bad either.
CHAD 1: Oh. So, what does that mean?
CHAD 2: I don't know.
CHAD 1: ...
CHAD 2: ...
CHAD 1: ...
CHAD 2: ...

(Chad 1 makes an offering.)

CHAD 1: Snow cone?

(Chad 1 looks into his bag and pulls out a snow cone on a stick that has seen better days.)

Melted snow cone? On a stick?

(They share the melted snow cone on a stick.

Chad 1 tentatively puts his hand on Chad 2's leg.

Chad 2 tentatively puts his hand on Chad 1's hand.)

CHAD 1: Frickin' tunnel of love, man.
CHAD 2: Frickin' tunnel of love.

(The tunnel ends and the stage fills with light as both Chads look forward, each a little nervous and a little ok.)

END OF PLAY

The Miracle of Birth

I love a fair. There is an actual Miracle of Birth Barn at the Minnesota State Fair. One year I saw a cow have a calf pulled from it by chains, the smell of funnel cake and corn dogs in the air. That was the inspiration for this play. I decided to set it at a county fair because it felt more interesting to have the characters know each other. There's a different level of performance people have when they're trying to play it cool in front of folks they see on a daily basis.

This is one of my favorite plays in this anthology. I've only seen a public reading of it once, and it filled my little playwright heart with so much joy to hear the actors and audience scream with laughter. That's about as good as it gets.

WHERE
The Miracle of Birth barn at a county fair in rural Minnesota. Chairs arranged like bleachers. Decorations implying a baby shower in a barn. In general, lots of red, white and blue.

WHEN
Today.

CHARACTERS
SUE
BILL
JIM
CHRISTINE
DORIS
CHIP
A FEW SPECTATORS

A NOTE ON THE TEXT
This play is set in rural Minnesota, and as such it's helpful if the characters speak with thick working-class MN accents reminiscent of *Fargo* or *Drop Dead Gorgeous*.

The Miracle of Birth Barn.

The sounds of chicks hatching.

A few spectators watch the births, which happen (unseen) where the audience is.

Jim announces with a small microphone from the sidelines.

JIM: The final chick is almost out of its shell. Here it comes. Here it comes.

(Jim continues to repeat "Here it comes" as Sue and Bill enter.

Sue carries a fancy hand basket and is very, very pregnant.)

SUE: Oh, the Miracle of Birth barn is just my favorite.
BILL: And a fitting place to be, now that we're, [wink] ya know.

(He makes a gesture indicating she's pregnant.)

SUE: What could you possibly [wink] be referring to [wink, wink]? Baby carrot on a stick?

(She pulls two baby carrots on sticks from her hand basket.

This is too cute to handle, and Bill cannot handle it.

Jim continues to repeat "Here it comes.")

BILL: Oh, Sue, how do you think of these things?
SUE: They just come to me.

(They eat baby carrots on a stick, but it takes them a while to actually do this because they're so giddy from how cute this all is.)

JIM: *(Having truly been saying "Here it comes" this whole time)* Here it comes. Fun fact: when a chicken hatches it's called "pipping," and it can take anywhere from one to twenty-four hours. But this lucky little guy's going to get some assistance from farmer Christine Lovdahl here. Hi, Christine. Here it comes. Here it comes. Gosh, it's kind of like that scene from *Jurassic Park*, isn't it?

CHRISTINE: *(Popping her head out, massaging an egg)* Except unlike a Velociraptor, we will be eating them instead of them eating us.

(Christine and Jim think this joke is beyond funny.)

JIM: That's a good one, Christine. A little Miracle of Birth barn humor for ya, folks. Almost there. Almost there. And there it is.

(Everyone applauds. Welcome to the world, little chickens!)

And that is the miracle of birth. Well done, chickens. And well done, farmer Christine Lovdahl. We're going to take a quick break and when we come back, Doris and Chip Stangler's cow, Petunia, will give birth to a calf.

(Everyone disburses.)

SUE: Ya know, Bill, watching these baby animals come into the world, it just fills ya with hope.

BILL: It sure does. These are dark times we're living in.

SUE: Real dark. Kind of feels like it's all going to hell in a hand basket.

BILL: Speaking of which, nice hand basket.

SUE: Thanks. Pier One. But, in spite of all that...sitting here today with you in the Miracle of Birth barn, expecting our own little miracle [wink] of birth [wink, wink]...I can't help but feel that everything is going to be ok, ya know?

BILL: Yah.

(They share a tender moment.

Jim walks over.)

JIM: Bill and Sue Laudenbach.

BILL: Good to see ya, Jim.

SUE: You're doin' a great job out there.

JIM: *(He knows)* Thanks.

SUE: How's Jake?

JIM: Oh, he's moved home, so. Kids. What are ya gonna do? Say, Sue, is it just me or do ya look a little different?

SUE: *(Loving it.)* ...What do ya mean?

JIM: Well, sitting there eating your baby carrots on a stick from your very fancy hand basket—

SUE: Pier One.

JIM: You kind of look like you're glowing. You get your haircut?

SUE: *(Giddy)* Yup. I got my haircut. That must be why I'm glowing. Baby corn? On a stick?

(Sue pulls three baby corns on sticks from her hand basket.

Bill and Sue are so giddy that it's hard to believe Jim isn't catching on to the fact that they're pregnant, but he's not. He's really not.

Jim is, however, picking up on their heightened energy, and he finds it a little odd. Odd things make him uncomfortable. He eats.)

JIM: These were always Jake's favorites when he was little. Back then anything seemed possible. Well, anything except him moving back home and living the rest of his adult life in my basement. But then, kids. Ya know?

(Jim inhales sharply. Is he going to cry? Then just as suddenly, he's normal again.)

Ohp, here come the Stanglers with their cow. Sue. Bill.

SUE & BILL: Jim.

(Jim returns to his announcer area.)

SUE: Was he crying?

BILL: I think it's a lot of pressure announcing events at a county fair.

SUE: Local celebrities: they're just like us, / but they're not.

BILL: But they're not, yah.

JIM: Everyone, please take your seats. Fun fact: when a cow loves another cow—or they've been put in the same pen by a farmer who could magically use a few more cows—their love produces a calf.

(Sue and Bill hold hands meaningfully. It is genuine and beautiful.)

And maybe this calf will grow up to be a steak, or maybe it'll be a brisket. Or maybe it'll end up going to one of them fancy liberal arts colleges where it'll double major in Fine Arts and Philosophy and then move home because its education cost more than it will earn for literally the rest of its life. Who knows? Life is very complicated. Doris and Chip, please bring in Petunia.

(Doris and Chip bring in Petunia.

So, let's be real: there isn't an actual cow and there definitely shouldn't be anyone dressed as one.

Maybe this is just us seeing Doris's and Chip's backs adjusting an imagined cow off stage. Maybe they're in a vom. Maybe everyone just looks out to the audience. Whatever it is, the cow itself isn't that important. However this is staged, it's best done in a way that allows us to focus on Sue's and Bill's journey.)

SUE: Just look at her, Bill. She looks so content, doesn't she?

JIM: Petunia went into active labor a while ago, and she is now fully dilated with contractions coming hard and fast.

(Petunia moos.)

BILL: Is content the word? She looks a little like she's in pain.

SUE: You can see it behind her eyes.

(Petunia moos sharply. She's definitely in pain.)

Very far behind her eyes. Baby back rib? On a stick?

(How fun! They eat their baby back ribs and end up getting a lot of BBQ sauce on their hands and faces. It is fun and not embarrassing.

Petunia moos throughout.

Sue is truly covered in BBQ sauce.)

Bill, can I tell you something? It's always been my dream to be a mom. I know that's maybe not the most cutting-edge thing to say, but I don't care. I can't wait to hold this little squidgy thing in my hands that's part me and part you, and also part of everyone that came before us, ya know? Going all the way back to the beginning.

BILL: Like to the dinosaurs?

SUE: Maybe not that far. But how incredible that our love can produce a person. And they'll go out into the world with your eyes and my nose, and your mom's ears, and your dad's eyebrows. Well, maybe not your dad's eyebrows. Those are kind of intense and maybe actually only one very large eyebrow. But some part of your dad that isn't distracting to look at will be there too. Or maybe it won't and that's actually probably ok. We'll love them, and they'll love us, and it'll be like we've done what we were put on this earth to do.

(Petunia lets out an intense, huge moo.)

JIM: Chip, can you spin Petunia around so the folks on the other side can see what's happening?

BILL: *(Covered in BBQ sauce)* You got a little something on your [face].

SUE: *(Wiping but not getting it)* Thanks. I guess what I'm trying to say is...there's no one I'd rather do this with. I love you so much, and I feel so lucky that we—oh my god that cow has two little hooves sticking out of its butt. Why are there two little hooves sticking out of its butt?

JIM: I know what you're thinking folks, why does Petunia have two little hooves sticking out of her butt...but it isn't her butt, it's her very, very dilated vagina, and soon a fully formed calf is gonna make its way out of that vagina and into our hearts. Fun fact: this calf is oversized, so getting it out is gonna be, what's the world, Doris?

DORIS: *(Popping her head out)* A lot.

JIM: Kids. Sometimes it's hard for them to leave your womb. Or your basement.

DORIS: I know what you mean. When I gave birth to my Sarah, she was so scared of being out in the world that she tried to crawl right back inside me.

JIM: That can't be true.

DORIS: It is. Doctor Merten said it's the only time he's seen it happen. It's in the Guinness Book of World Records. The family doesn't talk about it often, mostly 'cause we don't want the fame to go to our heads. Anyway, eventually the doctor was able to kind of claw my Sarah out and then it turned out she had these rage issues. Probably because she's not good at not getting what she wants. So, it was all screaming all the time. Just aah! AAAAAAAAH! And then she got to the sixth grade and it was time to pick an instrument, and she picked the piccolo. So, it was just screaming and piccolo. Screaming and piccolo. She's into cage fighting now, so maybe that'll be an outlet.

JIM: Oh, Doris.

DORIS: And Jesus thought he had it bad with that cross he had to bear. And don't get me started on Dustin.

CHIP: *(Popping his head out)* Don't get her started on Dustin.

DORIS: It's been a real unpleasant life we've had since having kids.

JIM: I know what you mean. My Jake's a—I'm not gonna say disappointment and embarrassment, but I'm stuck with him in my basement until probably the day I die. Or until the day I kill him.

(Petunia moos in pain.

Doris and Chip run off.

Sue and Bill suddenly don't look very well.)

SUE: Baby bottle of wine? No stick, but.

BILL: Please.

(They each open and down a single serving bottle of wine.)

You have any more?

SUE: I'm only allowed to have one.

BILL: What about me?

SUE: I thought we were in this together.

BILL: We are, I just.

SUE: What?

BILL: Nothing. I just.

SUE: YOU JUST WHAT?

BILL: Pretend I didn't say anything.

(Petunia moos intensely.)

JIM: Something's up. Doris is slipping her hands inside Petunia to check if everything is ok. How's she feel, Doris?

DORIS: I think we need chains.

JIM: Looks like we're gonna need chains, folks.

CHIP: Dustin, can you grab us some chains? Dustin? Dustin?

DORIS: Dustin!

CHIP: Dustin!

DORIS: Dustin!

CHIP: Dustin!

DORIS: Dustin!

JIM: Has anyone seen Dustin?

(Christine enters and sits behind Sue and Bill.)

CHRISTINE: I just heard him saying he was going to the gambling tent to buy pull tabs then take a trip to the cake walk.

CHIP: Pull tabs?!

(Doris pops out wearing very long, very messy birthing gloves.)

DORIS: The cake walk?! How many times do I gotta tell him sugar's like crack cocaine?! Where on earth did he get that money from?

CHIP: I didn't give it to him.

DORIS: Neither did I.

CHIP: Well, he had to get it from one of us.

DORIS: You better not be blaming me.

CHIP: Well, if he didn't get it from me and he didn't get it from you, then— oh no. My wallet. He stole my wallet, that son of a bitch.

DORIS: Don't you call me a bitch.

CHIP: That's not what I / meant.

DORIS: What are you doing just standing there? He's your son. Go find him and you bring him back here.

CHIP: Alright, I'm going.

DORIS: Go faster.

CHIP: I'm going faster.

DORIS: Why are you still here?

(Chip leaves. Doris acts as though nothing has happened.)

Kids. Guess I'll have to handle the chains myself.

(She exits.)

JIM: For those of you needing a break from the blood, hooves, and tears here in the cow pen, fun fact: crab spider babies survive by eating their mother alive, which is happening right now in the arachnid section of the barn.

(Doris passes through with two long chains in her hands.)

DORIS: Lucky her.

(She is gone.)

CHRISTINE: *(Innocently)* Is it just me or are things a little tense?

BILL: Apparently having children is not all it's cracked up to be.

CHRISTINE: Oh, well, like most things in life, it's a mixture of both positive and negative. It'd be foolish to go into it thinking it'll be perfect.

(To Bill)

You got a little something on your [face].

BILL: *(Wipes and misses)* Thanks.

SUE: *(A lightbulb)* Christine, you have a daughter.

CHRISTINE: I do, yah.

SUE: And she's a real nice girl.

CHRISTINE: That's so nice of you to say. Thank you. Rhoda's a good girl. She's real driven and good at getting what she wants.

BILL: You must be so proud.

CHRISTINE: I am. You hear "no" so much in life, and it can really get you down if you listen to it, ya know?

SUE: *(Agreeing)* Mmm.

CHRISTINE: But Rhoda, when she sets her mind to something, she makes it happen. She's real special.

(Sue and Bill are comforted by this.

They put their arms around each other.)

Of course, a lot of her classmates tend to keep their distance, especially that boy, Claude...before he drowned mysteriously at that school picnic. I recently found out he won a penmanship contest that Rhoda thought she should have won. Strange. And then there was that dog she begged us to buy her, but she got bored with it, and it accidentally fell out of that window. So weird. The maintenance man seemed to think Rhoda was behind it all, but he mysteriously was burned alive on his mattress. Don't tell anyone, but sometimes I worry Rhoda is a bad...what's the word?

SUE: Apple?

CHRISTINE: No. It's on the tip of my tongue. Like a little thing that you plant, and life grows from it?

BILL: A bad nut?

CHRISTINE: It'll come to me. You don't think I should be worried, do you?

(Doris enters and gives ponchos to everyone.)

JIM: Looks like we're going to have a splash zone, folks.

DORIS: Since Chip is off finding our good-for-nothing son, would anyone be willing to help me?

SUE: You know what, Bill? I think it's / time to [go].

BILL: Yeah, why don't we [leave]?

(Sue and Bill stand up to leave.

Jim and Doris completely misread their standing and think it means they're volunteering.)

JIM: Sue and Bill Laundenbach! That's so nice!

(Doris hands them each a very long chain that stretches off stage.

They are horrified.)

DORIS: I'm gonna tie these to the calf's feet and you're gonna help me walk it out. Just don't pull 'til I tell ya, otherwise—not to be dramatic—it'll be total carnage.

JIM: You can always count on Sue and Bill, can't ya? Let's give them a big round of applause.

(The audience applauds.

Christine pats them on the shoulders, but they don't want her to touch them, this woman who has mothered pure evil.)

SUE: Bill, I don't think I can do this.

BILL: Please don't make me pull the chains alone.

SUE: No. I don't know if I can be a parent.

BILL: Me either.

DORIS: We're all set. Walk it out!

(Sue and Bill gently walk out the unseen cow with their chains and have the most intense conversation ever that no one else seems to be aware of them having.)

SUE: And for me, it's not even about if our kid is evil.

BILL: That is 100% what I'm worried about.

SUE: Well, there is that. But what on earth is worth this? You go through all that pain, and, for what? So this little thing that clawed out of you hooves first can ruin your life?

DORIS: Walk a little harder!

(Sue and Bill walk their chains a bit more intentionally.)

SUE: What about me? I was supposed to go to Paris and learn French. I've still never even been out of Minnesota.

DORIS: Harder! Harder!

(They pull with even more intention.)

SUE: Am I supposed to give up what I wanted in life because I've got this little demon with my father-in-law's giant, single eyebrow?

BILL: Hey.

SUE: Remember when I said all these babies fill me with hope? That was a lie. You're married to a liar.

JIM: There's the head.

SUE: How can I feel hope? Have you seen the world?! I can't inflict this on an innocent child. It'll steamroll them like it steamrolled us.

DORIS: Don't slow down! Don't slow down!

BILL: What if we went home and boarded up all the windows and doors, crawled into bed, and just disappeared?

SUE: Could we actually do that?

BILL: It's called denial. It worked for my parents; they've been together for thirty years.

DORIS: KEEP PULLING!

SUE: I can put on the cute bed sheets!

BILL: And we can just watch baking shows!

JIM: Here it comes.

SUE: We'll never have to leave!

BILL: We'll never have to deal with anything.

SUE: We'll never have to deal with anything.

DORIS: PULL!

SUE: It'll be just us.

BILL: Happy.

SUE: Safe.

> *(As if on cue, Petunia lets out a climactic moo.*
>
> *The splatter zone is splashed with birthing fluid.*
>
> *Or maybe it's just a sound cue and mimed reactions.*
>
> *But, in the million-dollar production, it's a lot of birthing fluid that magically seems to come from nowhere.*
>
> *Applause from the spectators.)*

JIM: And that is the miracle of birth. Just look at that calf, folks. It has its mother's beautiful spots and its grandfather's thick, single eyebrow. How sweet.

CHRISTINE: You two did great!

SUE & BILL: Thanks.

CHRISTINE: *(Re: a text)* Oh, I'd better go! Rhoda needs me immediately.

> *(She texts.)*

"Sure, honey, I'll meet you on the roof." Maybe she's not such a bad, uh, whatever after all.

BILL: A bad egg?
CHRISTINE: [No] It'll come to me.

(She is gone.

Chip has returned, no sign of Dustin.

Chip and Doris loudly improvise an argument about their son that they inexplicably seem to think is private as:)

JIM: We're going to take a quick break folks, during which I'm going to run home and make sure my son—who has a fancy liberal arts degree in Fine Arts and Philosophy but doesn't know how to cook or do his own laundry—hasn't burned down the house leaving me with literally nothing. When we return, we'll watch Fran Bunkowski's exotic Surinam toad, which will give birth out of its back.

(Jim starts to leave. As he goes:)

Sue, you really do look like you're glowing. You both do.
BILL: ...Maybe it's the fluid?
JIM: I just can't put my finger on it. I'm gonna get you some towels.

(He is gone. Doris and Chip have left.)

SUE: Baby food?

(Sue pulls out a jar of actual baby food.)

BILL: You do love a theme.
SUE: I do.

(They eat the baby food. It doesn't taste as good as they want it to, but it's not bad either. Maybe it's kind of ok.

Seeing each other's expressions, they begin to laugh. A lot. This can take a second. It deflates the tension, and they feel like two people brought together by a shared traumatic experience. They truly love each other.)

BILL: You got something on your [face].

SUE: *(Laughing)* Thanks.
BILL: It'll be fine.
SUE: It'll be fine.
BILL: It'll be fine.
SUE: It will be fine.

(The hold their hands on her belly, both uncertain and hopeful.)

BILL: My God, it is pretty incredible, isn't it? Wow, it's kicking.
SUE: Um. Actually. I think my. I think my water broke.
BILL: ...Really?
SUE: Yeah.
BILL: Uh, somebody help! Help! Baby! BABY!

(Doris and Chip rush over and attend to Sue as Jim re-enters with towels.

He returns to his mic.)

JIM: Folks, change of plans. The toad will have to wait. We have a Miracle of Birth Barn first: a human baby.

(Oohs and Aahs from the crowd.)

DORIS: Good thing I still got my gloves on.
JIM: This is why I love the fair: the drama.

(Sue has an intensely painful contraction.)

Now let's all sit back, relax, and welcome Sue and Bill Laudenbach to the wonderful world of parenthood.

(Everyone gathers around Sue. Some helping, some gawking.

It is somehow sweet, funny and disturbing.

Sue reacts verbally to another painful contraction.

A Random Person takes a photo or two with their phone.

Chip spots an unseen Dustin.)

CHIP: Dustin! There you are! Give me back my wallet, you piece of.

>	*(Chip is gone.*

>	*Sue has another verbal reaction to a painful contraction.*

>	*Bill takes her hand.)*

BILL: You're doing great. You're doing great.
SUE: I don't feel great.
BILL: That's ok. You're still doing great.

>	*(Sue continues to push. She and Bill are terrified, but hopeful.)*

END OF PLAY

Eat Cake

Lindsay and Jen's apartment, Bushwick. Clean…but maybe not that clean.

WHEN
Tonight.

CHARACTERS
LINDSAY – 20s/30s. A virtuous and clean roommate. Makes great cake.
JEN – 20s/30s. A virtuous and messy roommate. Loves great cake.

A NOTE ON THE TEXT
The dialogue in this play really wants to fly. These characters are clever and think quickly on their toes.

Let the passive aggression here be gloriously aggressive.

Lindsay and Jen at home.

Lindsay holds an immaculate slice of cake. Like, wow, we the audience are so impressed by this treat that looks too good to eat.

LINDSAY: Cake?

JEN: It's beautiful.

LINDSAY: Thanks. Please.

JEN: I couldn't.

LINDSAY: I made it myself.

JEN: You're so thoughtful.

LINDSAY: Stop it, you're the thoughtful one.

JEN: You're just saying that.

LINDSAY: I am saying it, but only because I mean it. You give up your seat to anyone who might need it on the subway, even if they aren't hobbling or pregnant. And you, like, call people out for saying insensitive things, but you do it in a way that's super kind and doesn't make them feel like garbage even if the implications of their viewpoints are that they are actual garbage. It's so inspiring.

JEN: Stop it, you know I don't do compliments.

LINDSAY: But it's true! You're a saint. A nondenominational saint.

JEN: You are.

LINDSAY: You are.

JEN: You are.

LINDSAY: Please have some cake.

JEN: Well, if you insist.

(They share the cake. It's delicious. Lindsay is a cake-making God.

They eat the cake throughout the rest of the scene. And right now, Jen's mouth is stuffed.)

Holy shit. Jesus. Wow.

LINDSAY: It's not me. It's a recipe from a book I bought directly from the chef who focuses on sustainability and community through her self-published cookbooks. All of the proceeds go to ethical charities, even though I think she herself might be super poor.

JEN: Wow.

LINDSAY: Or, like, she presents as poor, even though she's not, out of solidarity.

JEN: Amazing.

LINDSAY: Anyway, now that we're here for this house meeting.

JEN: Oh, is this a meeting?

LINDSAY: Only if you want it to be. I don't want to make any assumptions.

JEN: Uh-huh.

LINDSAY: Just that we're here and being mindful of not wanting to abuse your time later...

JEN: Sure.

LINDSAY: Because I know you're, like, super busy with everything. And you're doing an incredible job balancing it all. Truly. Like, when people talk about people who should be running the world, they're talking about you. And not, like, in an authoritarian way. No, I mean you're an amazing leader in an inspiring, radical, liberal arts syllabus kind of way, you know?

JEN: *(Polite but sharp)* Is there something you wanted to ask me?

LINDSAY: Would you be open to a maybe kind of slightly uncomfortable request?

JEN: Do more of your extended friend and family network want to stay with us when they visit?

LINDSAY: No.

JEN: Oh, thank god!

LINDSAY: Not that it's a problem to house my loved ones when they're on vacation.

JEN: Right, of course.

LINDSAY: New York is very expensive.

JEN: It's built on economic injustice.

LINDSAY: Exactly. And therefore, my extended friend and family network will always be allowed to stay with us when they visit.

JEN: Right.

LINDSAY: So, anyway, my first question.

JEN: ...There are multiple issues?

LINDSAY: No issues, only questions. My first one: we're out of toilet paper. You use a lot of toilet paper.

JEN: Sorry, what's the question?

LINDSAY: Are you ok?

JEN: I'm fine.

LINDSAY: Oh good! Just wanted to make sure. 'Cause we're out of toilet paper.

JEN: Do you want me to buy some more?

LINDSAY: I don't want you to do anything.

JEN: ...Should I buy some more?

LINDSAY: Thank you for offering. That's so kind. You totally don't have to, but I'm grateful for your generosity.

JEN: Uh, no problem.

LINDSAY: And question two: I guess I'm just wondering if you'd be open to discussing, how do I put this nicely? Would you be open to discussing the possibility of taking your hair out of the drain when you shower?

JEN: ...

LINDSAY: And I don't mean that in a way that's, like, commenting on the amount of hair on your body or the rate at which it sheds. I champion you being you. It's just a lot of you. So, if you're cool to take it out of the drain and throw it away or at least in the toilet, that would be amazing. Not that I, like, think you or anything that used to be a part of you should be in a toilet, but it just might be nice to remember the shower is a shared space and we should all leave it better than we found it, like the Scouts. Not that I condone any of the myriad problems the Scouts have had in the. I just. Can you please be a little more courteous when it comes to your hair?

JEN: Wow. I didn't realize I was not being courteous.

LINDSAY: I don't want to offend you.

JEN: I'm totally not offended, and I'm totally not going to cry.

LINDSAY: Great.

(Offended, Jen shovels cake into her mouth).

JEN: *(Hate eating)* First of all, I hear you. I acknowledge my misstep and the pain it's caused you.

LINDSAY: Oh no. I think I may have—

JEN: I applaud the courage you've had to say something. I applaud you. I will strive to be better in the future. We're all learning, right?

LINDSAY: Look, uh—

JEN: And speaking of being better: maybe you could do the dishes once or ever.

LINDSAY: Could we not distract from the issue at hand or try to hurt with our words?

JEN: I'm sorry the act of me living my life is preventing you from living yours.

LINDSAY: It's not! But it is preventing the water from draining, so—

JEN: My apologies for oppressing you by making you feel like you're living with a wildebeest—

LINDSAY: If you identify as a wildebeest, I celebrate your coming out. I can make another cake.

JEN: ...

LINDSAY: That was a joke. To lighten the [mood].

(By now, there should be one bite of cake left. Each is too polite to eat it. They periodically shove the plate toward the other one as a way of indicating they should have the last bite.)

JEN: It's yours.

LINDSAY: No, it's yours.

JEN: You know what? I will happily remove my clearly disgusting-to-you self from the drain.

LINDSAY: I'm sorry. You don't have to.

JEN: I want to.

LINDSAY: I shouldn't have said anything.

JEN: I'm glad you did. You handled this in a really sensitive, adult way.

LINDSAY: Have some more frosting.

JEN: To show you how much this doesn't negatively affect me, I'm going to pull the hair out of the drain right now.

LINDSAY: Please, it can wait.

JEN: Please, it can't. I'll pull it out right now. With my teeth.

LINDSAY: You really don't have to—

JEN: I gently suggest that, yes, it would be the most appropriate way to clarify for all involved how disrespectful me being a human being with hair truly is.

LINDSAY: I'm sorry.

JEN: No, I'm sorry.

LINDSAY: Except I really am.

JEN: Are you questioning my sincerity?

LINDSAY: Never!

JEN: Because that would be very not nice.

LINDSAY: Look: I'm sorry I brought this up.

JEN: I'm sorry you had to in the first place.

LINDSAY: Listen, it was hurtful and offensive and. I've had a long week. I know, we all have. But I hate my job. Again, I know. Who doesn't? But mine is slowly pulling my soul out of my belly button. I'm dying inside. Maybe I'm already dead. I cried on the train today. Twice.

JEN: Oh God.

LINDSAY: So, I'm sorry. All I wanted to do was take a shower and not have to dig into the drain first.

JEN: I'm sorry.

LINDSAY: No. I am. And I'm a terrible roommate. I'm trash. I'm trash.

(Lindsay continues to intone "I'm trash" as she does something loud that completely degrades herself. Maybe she screams into her hands. Maybe she bangs her head on the table. Maybe she slaps herself a few times. Maybe she pulls out clumps of her own hair. Have fun, dear performer.

It builds until it becomes unbearably uncomfortable. We're watching a person reach their most humiliated, vulnerable low point.

Whatever Lindsay does, it should be so horrific to watch that Jen earnestly says:)

JEN: I'm the asshole. I'll take my hair out of the drain.

LINDSAY: *(Same energy as top of play, as though her fit didn't happen)* Thanks! And, if you could do it right now that would be amazing, because I was hoping to hop into the shower right after our convo.

(Jen sees what Lindsay did there and as sweetly as possible says:)

JEN: Cool. I will happily clean the drain.

LINDSAY: Thank you.

JEN: ...After you have the last bite of cake.

LINDSAY: I couldn't. It's for you.

JEN: Please.

LINDSAY: Please.

JEN: Please.

LINDSAY: Fine, I'll throw it out.

JEN: People are starving. You should have it.

LINDSAY: You should have it. People who identify as wildebeests should feel cared for.

JEN: I don't identify as a wildebeest, but the sugar most certainly probably contributes to my hair loss. Please enjoy.

LINDSAY: It's rude for a chef to finish their own food.

JEN: You've lived in this apartment longer than me. I don't want it to seem like I'm colonizing your cake.

LINDSAY: I invited you to have it. It'd actually be rude not to eat the cake.

JEN: It'd be rude to make me feel guilty for not eating it.

LINDSAY: It'd be rude to say I'm rude. You're the one leaving your hair in the drain.

JEN: I'm not doing it on purpose.

LINDSAY: Well, maybe you should be more purposeful with your actions.

JEN: Should I purposefully shave my head so I'm less of an inconvenience to you?

LINDSAY: Eat the cake.

JEN: You eat the cake.

LINDSAY: Eat it.

JEN: Eat it.

LINDSAY: EAT THE CAKE.

(Lindsay shoves the last bite of cake into Jen's mouth.

Both are surprised by the aggression of it.)

Please.

(Both are surprised by themselves in general. And really embarrassed.

Jen chews.)

LINDSAY: Well, now I feel bad.

JEN: I'm going to go, and. Thank you for the cake.

LINDSAY: Thank YOU / for cleaning the.

JEN: By the way, would you mind if I had some friends over tonight?

LINDSAY: I work early tomorrow.

JEN: How early?

LINDSAY: Early.

JEN: ...

LINDSAY: But sure.

JEN: They're experimental drummers.

LINDSAY: Great.

JEN: We'll try not to keep you up.

LINDSAY: That's so kind of you.

JEN: You're the kind one.

LINDSAY: Don't forget to pay the gas bill.

JEN: Thanks again for the cake.

LINDSAY: Uh-huh.

END OF PLAY

Mr. Brown

WHERE

Dylan's eclectic, messy apartment in Minneapolis. Low-cost seating—maybe a bean bag chair or camping chairs. Christmas lights on the floor (unplugged). Empty pizza boxes. This place feels young.

WHEN

Tonight.

CHARACTERS

DYLAN – Early 20s. A recent college graduate. Open, eager, bold.
STEVEN – Mid 30s. An elementary school teacher. Thoughtful, cautious, reluctant.

A NOTE ON THE TEXT

Though this play is set in Minnesota, I think leaning into the accent would be more distracting than helpful. It's likely best played with general American accents.

Moonlight.

Steven and Dylan in the throes of passion.

Steven pulls away.

STEVEN: Sorry. I don't think I can do this.

DYLAN: Is it because I'm a man?

STEVEN: No.

DYLAN: Is it because you were my second-grade teacher?

STEVEN: Yup. That is. Yup.

DYLAN: That was forever ago! I was seven years old.

STEVEN: Oh God. I feel dirty.

DYLAN: In a good way?

STEVEN: No!

DYLAN: I'm twenty-one now! I don't have that bowl cut. I have all my adult teeth. There's nothing wrong with what we're doing.

STEVEN: I need to leave.

DYLAN: Why? I've always liked you. You taught me basic math.

STEVEN: Gah!

DYLAN: And actually, if it helps to think about this mathematically, twenty-one is greater than eighteen which is waaaay greater than seven. What we're doing is not illegal.

STEVEN: Not technically.

DYLAN: I'm a consenting adult. I'm here because I want to be. And I could care less that you're super old now.

STEVEN: ...I'm sorry, what?

DYLAN: What?

STEVEN: I'm not old.

DYLAN: That's the spirit. Age is just a number.

STEVEN: I'm not old. I'm thirty-five.

DYLAN: I thought you were, like, fifty?

STEVEN: Excuse you.

DYLAN: A good looking fifty! Like, you look really good for fifty.

STEVEN: I'm not fifty!

DYLAN: Wait, so if you're thirty-five now, that means you were?

STEVEN: I was twenty-one when I was. When I was [your teacher]—

DYLAN: Oh my God that's the same age I am now!

STEVEN: I'm going to be sick.

DYLAN: Oh God! Getting with someone fourteen years younger than me is—Gross! Nope!

STEVEN: Because they're seven!

DYLAN: That's so young!

STEVEN: Yes!

DYLAN: That's too young!

STEVEN: Exactly!

DYLAN: What are we even doing?

STEVEN: I don't know!

(A beat.)

DYLAN: You want to try again?

STEVEN: No!

(Steven gathers his things.)

DYLAN: We were having such a nice night.

STEVEN: Until you called me Mr. Brown.

DYLAN: Sorry, it was just. It was a lightbulb moment. You mentioned you loved *A Little Life* and I said it was one of my favorite books, and you smiled and the whole room just. It lit up. I thought, what an incredible smile. Beautiful. Kind. There's something about it. And also something kind of familiar. Like, why is it so familiar? Then I realized: it's Mr. Brown. That's the smile he had when I finally learned how to read.

STEVEN: And on that note. Thank you for the drinks. And thank you for a memorable evening that after all of this whiskey I will hopefully forget.

DYLAN: That's it?

STEVEN: Yup.

DYLAN: ...but you told me I was smart.

STEVEN: Because you were. You are.

DYLAN: Most people think I'm just this fun time party boy, but you actually...

(Small pause.)

Steven, I'm lonely. I feel so alone. And talking with you, I just...I feel like someone is seeing me—the actual me—for the first time.

STEVEN: Look, Dylan, I didn't go to The Saloon expecting to make a real connection with someone. You're really thoughtful. The way you unpack politics? It's so nuanced. And your ideas about American identity are really. They're amazing. Honestly, if I were your age, you would be waaaaay out of my league.

(Dylan moves closer to Steven.)

DYLAN: Well, it's a good thing you're not.

(Steven pulls away.)

STEVEN: I was your chaperone on the field trip to the zoo where you wet your pants.

DYLAN: Can we not / go there?

STEVEN: We worked on capital letters the morning after your parents told you they were getting a divorce. If I knew it was you, I never would have let tonight happen the way it did.

DYLAN: ...

(Steven is at the door.)

STEVEN: Well. This was, um. You've grown into a. You're a really cool young man. I wish you, uh. I wish you the best.

DYLAN: Wait! Look, we don't have to, you know. We could just...?

STEVEN: ....

DYLAN: Night cap?

STEVEN: ....

DYLAN: No strings attached.

STEVEN: ...

DYLAN: ...

STEVEN: Do you have anything that's not whiskey?

DYLAN: There's some Malibu or Smirnoff Ice in the?

STEVEN: ...

DYLAN: That was a joke. Beer?

STEVEN: ...
DYLAN: ...
STEVEN: Sure.

(*Dylan disappears into another room and almost immediately returns.*)

DYLAN: Forgot to tell you my roommate is home, so if you could keep it, you know.

(*Dylan is gone.*

Steven takes a look around the dark room.

He tries to find a light switch but cannot.

He's really trying.

Like, is there actually light in this room?

Dylan pops his head in.)

Oh, yeah, sorry, there are no overhead lights. We keep saying we should buy a lamp or two, but we just haven't. I guess we're both kind of waiting for the other to finally do it. Like vacuuming. Or doing the dishes. There are Christmas lights if you want to.

(*Dylan points at a string of lights on the ground.*

Steven plugs them in. They give the room a lovely glow.)

Kind of romantic.

(*Dylan exits.*

Satisfied, Steven walks toward the beanbag or camping chair.

He trips on a few pizza boxes on the floor.

He sits and takes a moment to get situated.

Mr. Brown could not feel older.)

Dylan re-enters with two beers. They both have mint sprigs sticking out of the openings.)

Aw, this is nice. Cheers.

STEVEN: What's this?

DYLAN: It's a garnish.

STEVE: For a beer?

DYLAN: I thought it'd feel fancy. It's fresh mint.

STEVE: Cheers.

(They drink. They gag.)

DYLAN: Oh, there's a little soil in mine.

STEVE: Yup.

DYLAN: Sorry.

(Steven begins to laugh.

Dylan feels self-conscious, but then he too thinks this whole thing is hilarious.

They laugh together for a few beats. The awkwardness melts away until their eyes meet, and things become tentative. Vulnerable. More first love.)

STEVEN: ...

DYLAN: ...

STEVEN: ...

DYLAN: ...

STEVEN: ...

DYLAN: ...

STEVEN: ...

DYLAN: So, am I the first student you've gone home with?

STEVEN: Uh, yup. Yup.

DYLAN: *(Touched)* Aw.

STEVEN: Am I the first teacher you've brought home?

DYLAN: Yeah. Well, technically, yeah. I did hook up with my Calc professor, but we went to *his* place, so. Oh! Don't worry! I wasn't his student at the time either. We randomly found each other on Grindr and it was weird but then it wasn't.

STEVEN: You have a thing for older men?

DYLAN: I have a thing for mature minds.

STEVEN: *(Flirty?)* Oh really?

DYLAN: *(Flirty)* Oh really. You're more than just a pretty face, Mr. Brown.

STEVEN: Please don't.

DYLAN: Oh God. Sorry.

STEVEN: See, it was nice until.

DYLAN: That just came out. Sorry. Steven. You are hot. Steven. I like talking with you. Steven. I'm going to stop calling you Mr. Brown. Steven.

(Dylan coyly tussles Steven's hair.)

STEVEN: ...

DYLAN: ...

STEVEN: ...

DYLAN: ...

(Suddenly, Steven downs the rest of his beer in one gulp.)

STEVEN: Well, I should, uh, I should hop on the bus. Thanks for the beer.

(He starts to leave.)

DYLAN: Where did you go?

STEVEN: ???

DYLAN: The year after you taught me. You left the school. Where'd you go?

STEVEN: Oh, uh. The school found out I was gay and some parents had, uh. They didn't want me teaching their kids. So I had to, uh. That's how I ended up in Minneapolis.

DYLAN: Sorry.

STEVEN: *(At the door)* Thanks. Yeah, people have, uh. People talk.

(Small pause.)

People talk.

DYLAN: Stay.

STEVEN: I really can't.

DYLAN: Is that because that's what you want or what you feel like you're supposed to do?

STEVEN: Dylan, it's complicated.

DYLAN: The world is so much weirder than this.

(Pause.)

We could take it slow.

STEVEN: That would be nice, but.

DYLAN: But what? It's not like we have to get married. This is a first date.

STEVEN: ...Is this a date?

DYLAN: I don't know. ...Is it?

(Pause.)

Remember when you read us *The Very Hungry Caterpillar*?

STEVEN: Goodnight, Dylan.

DYLAN: We could have a really beautiful butterfly here. We just need to give it a chance.

STEVEN: ...

DYLAN: ...

STEVEN: ...

DYLAN: ...

STEVEN: ...

DYLAN: ...

STEVEN: ...

DYLAN: ...

STEVEN: ...

DYLAN: ...

(Blackout.)

END OF PLAY

The Long-Distance Thing

A quiet coffee shop with an impeccable playlist in Brooklyn. The sort of place where the entire staff probably have strong opinions about what is and is not cool.

WHEN

This afternoon.

CHARACTERS

NICK – 20s/30s. American. Lives in New York. A Do-er.

OSCAR – 20s/30s. Not American. Lives in his home country. Anxious. You're welcome to lightly tailor Oscar's vocabulary to best suit the actor you cast. He could be from an English-speaking country or speak English as a second language with an American cadence. The important thing is he is not American. Whatever you decide, please make a choice that is thoughtful and specific.

Oscar sits at a table in a hipster coffee shop. He fidgets nervously.

Nick enters with two coffees.

NICK: *(Sarcastic)* Barista with the beard loves his job. Do you think they only hire mean people?

(Nick sets down their coffees.)

OSCAR: Thanks.

NICK: Lady Rizzo's performing at Joe's Pub this weekend, if you want to, or there's that weird installation at MoMa, or. I mean, normally you're off the plane with a whole itinerary, so you tell me.

OSCAR: ...

NICK: Are you ok?

OSCAR: Mhmm.

NICK: You look sort of.

OSCAR: Must be the jet lag.

NICK: You're sweating.

OSCAR: No, I'm not.

NICK: You're, like, sopping wet.

OSCAR: ...

NICK: Oscar?

OSCAR: ...

NICK: ...

(Oscar dabs himself with napkins.)

OSCAR: I can't, um.

NICK: ...

OSCAR: I can't do this anymore.

NICK: ...

OSCAR: ...

NICK: I. Ok. Wow.

OSCAR: *(Still dabbing)* Do you mind if I use your [napkin]?

(He dabs with Nick's napkin in addition to the one he already has.)

What are you, uh. What are you thinking?

NICK: Um.

OSCAR: ...

NICK: I mean, I guess I had a feeling this might be coming.

OSCAR: Really?

NICK: The long-distance thing is tricky. And you haven't really looked me in the eye since you landed.

OSCAR: It's been on my mind for a while. I thought it was important to have this conversation in person.

NICK: Please stop dabbing.

OSCAR: Do you think water might help?

NICK: No.

(Oscar pulls up the bottom of his shirt and wipes his face)

OSCAR: I'm sorry.

NICK: *(Re: Shirt)* It's fine. The barista can't judge us anymore than he already has.

OSCAR: Look, we only see each other twice a year.

NICK: And online.

OSCAR: It's not the same.

NICK: It'd have been a lot harder a hundred years ago.

OSCAR: It's still hard. We live in different countries.

NICK: I know!

OSCAR: This just isn't sustainable.

NICK: I can text more. I can, I can—do you want me to leave you voice messages every day, or?

OSCAR: I think I need to use the dryer in the bathroom. I'll be right back.

NICK: You can't just drop something like that then run off.

OSCAR: Are you happy?

NICK: ...What?

OSCAR: Are you happy with this setup?

NICK: ...

OSCAR: Because I feel like there's a hole inside me. And the only way to not have it eat away at me is to keep moving. Clean my apartment. Go to the gym. Work late. Come home. Clean more. I have to outrun it, because if I stop...if I stop and let myself think about it, then I fall into it. I fall into the hole, and I just...I used to think eventually I'd hit the bottom...but now I'm not sure there even is one.

NICK: ...

OSCAR: We can't live like this. It's not fair to either of us.

NICK: I know, but—

OSCAR: And I've reached a point where I can't. I can't do this anymore. So, I guess this is my way of saying—

NICK: NO.

OSCAR: ...No?

NICK: We will make it work.

OSCAR: How?

NICK: If we set our minds to it, we can do anything.

OSCAR: You are so American.

NICK: I know!

OSCAR: That's not how it works in the rest of the world. That's maybe not even how it works here.

NICK: Do you love me?

OSCAR: Nick.

NICK: Do you love me?

OSCAR: YES!

NICK: Then what is the problem?

OSCAR: We can't go on like this.

NICK: I love you so much. So much! You live rent free in my head, like, 90% of the day. I get the mail and I think, 'What's Oscar doing right now?' Or I'll be catering some event where everyone's taking themselves way too seriously and I'll think, 'God, I wish Oscar was here so we could laugh at these weirdos.' And then at night! At night I lay in bed and I feel so alone. More alone than when I was single, because why aren't you there? You should be there. I just want to hold you and feel you next to me knowing that it's. That it's all going to be ok. That the pain and the fear and the, the everything. That it's all going to be ok.

OSCAR: ...

NICK: So, please don't.

OSCAR: But—

NICK: Please. Just please. Please don't break up with me.

OSCAR: ...

NICK: Please.

OSCAR: ...

NICK: ...

OSCAR: ...I'm sorry, what?

NICK: ???

OSCAR: ???

NICK: Please don't break up with me?

OSCAR: I'm not breaking up with you.

NICK: ???

OSCAR: I normally don't sweat so much. This is really embarrassing.

NICK: ???

OSCAR: I think we should stop the long-distance thing.

NICK: ???

OSCAR: I think we should live together.

NICK: Oh. OH.

OSCAR: Sorry, I—

NICK: No, you don't have to, / uh.

OSCAR: I could have been / more.

NICK: I'm such / a.

OSCAR: That was quite cryptic in retrospect.

NICK: It really was.

OSCAR: So, do you?

NICK: I'm an idiot.

OSCAR: No, I am.

NICK: I'm so stupid.

OSCAR: Do you want to live together?

NICK: Yes.

OSCAR: You do?

NICK: YES!

OSCAR: ...

NICK: ...

OSCAR: ...

NICK: ...Does this mean we're engaged?

OSCAR: A marriage visa would probably make the most [sense].

NICK: Uh.

OSCAR: Unless you don't think.

NICK: No, I do. I do.

OSCAR: Right.

(An explosion of hugs, kisses, joy.)

NICK: OH MY GOD!

OSCAR: EEE!

NICK: THIS IS SO!

OSCAR: YEAH!

NICK: It's totally not how I pictured it would be!

OSCAR: Same!

NICK: But you're the one who brought it up!

OSCAR: I know!

NICK: You're so wet.

OSCAR: Yeah. Wow. Sorry! I should give you a ring.

NICK: You don't have to

OSCAR: I want to. Or at least something to tide us over until we get the real. Here, uh.

(Oscar pulls of his watch.)

NICK: No, don't give me your watch.

OSCAR: It's a similar shape.

NICK: Who would you be if you weren't the only person our age who still wore one?

OSCAR: It's a wedding ring for Christ's sake.

NICK: ...

OSCAR: It looks nice on you.

NICK: I feel like I should give you something too! Uh. I don't really have, uh. I mean, there's my keys or my travel card? You're obviously the bread winner.

OSCAR: Ha.

NICK: Take my key ring.

OSCAR: But, sweetie, your bar code for CVS.

NICK: Shut up.

OSCAR: I really love you.

NICK: I really love you too.
OSCAR: Let's toast!
NICK: Yeah!

(They raise their coffee cups.)

OSCAR: Farewell, long-distance thing.
NICK: May she rest in peace.

(They drink.

They settle for a few beats, mystified and gleeful that this is actually happening.)

OSCAR: Now, there's just one more thing to talk about.
NICK: Should I ask the mean barista if he has a towel?
OSCAR: Shut up.
NICK: Or a fan?
OSCAR: No, but yes, but also...Who's making the move?

END OF PLAY

Snake Balls in Your Basement

WHERE

Pam and Ted's lawn in the very, very, very, very, very small town of Cold Lake, Minnesota. Fresh cut grass. Flowerbeds. The occasional horsefly or mosquito.

WHEN

Summer 1996.

CHARACTERS

PAM – 30s/40s. A person who is deeply uncomfortable in her own body and suddenly feels a new lease on life. This is the same Pam who appears in *Here on a Sunday*.

LORNA – 30s/40s. Pam's sister. Pessimistic, conservative, traditionalist.

TED – 30s/40s. Pam's husband. Nice but aloof.

A NOTE ON THE TEXT

This play is set in rural Minnesota, and as such it's helpful if the characters speak with thick working-class MN accents reminiscent of *Fargo* or *Drop Dead Gorgeous*.

PREMIERE

Snake Balls in your Basement was originally performed as part of *From Cold Lake: Episode 2*, which received its world premiere at The Peoples Improv Theater (Ali Reza Farahnakian, Founder and Caretaker; Stephen Stout, Artistic Director) in New York City on September 12th, 2016. The producers were Matt Cox, Kristin McCarthy Parker and Stephen Stout. It was directed by Colin Waitt. Songs and Score were composed by Tommy Crawford. Sound design & mixing was by Matt Cox. The cast was as follows:

PAM: Courtney Roche
LORNA: Nikki Coble

Pam lays on a towel in the sun. She wears a bikini that's sexy in a Minnesota in the 90s sort of way...so the waistline is probably very high and there are lots of polka dots.

She lounges like she's someone in the process of discovering the beauty of their own body.

Lorna enters, dour.

PAM: Howdy, stranger! Big day at Shopko?
LORNA: I think I'm getting carpal tunnel from folding all them tube tops.

(Lorna notices Pam.)

You got a haircut.
PAM: You like it?
LORNA: *(No)* It's different.

(Pam is insulted.)

PAM: Wine cooler?
LORNA: Ok.
PAM: They're passion fruit.
LORNA: Ooo!
PAM: I know! Fun!

(They crack open two wine coolers, toast and sip.

It tastes terrible.)

PAM: Huh.
LORNA: Now, that's really different.
PAM: Very different.
LORNA: Passion fruit, you said?
PAM: *(Another sip)* Mmm.
LORNA: Is that what passion tastes like?
PAM: The second sip is better.
LORNA: One was enough for me.
PAM: Actually, it kind of grows on you.

(Pam enjoys another sip.)

LORNA: You need some sunblock.
PAM: Maybe I want a tan.
LORNA: For who?
PAM: For me. And for...

(Small pause.)

LORNA: ...For Ted?
PAM: What?
LORNA: For your husband, Ted?
PAM: ...
LORNA: Do my back?

(Pam applies lotion to Lorna's back.

She quietly debates something.)

PAM: ...Lorna?   LORNA: You hear they found a
                                          buyer for the farm?

PAM (CON'T): What?
LORNA: Yah. Don Mausman and Gary Johnson were talking about a
    housing development. But Lucy Rolfhauser is pretty sure it'll be a
    mall.
PAM: All the way out here?
LORNA: I think they're thinking all the way out here won't be all the way
    out here much longer, if you know what I mean.
PAM: Our family farm: the site of a Waldenbooks and K.B. Toys.
LORNA: I guess that's progress.
PAM: I guess that's progress, yah.
LORNA: Were you gonna say something?
PAM: ???
LORNA: You said my name a minute ago.
PAM: Did I?
LORNA: Maybe you oughta slow down on the wine coolers.

(They lay out.

Pam thinks very, very hard about how to say something. Finally:)

PAM: The, uh. The Waltzes are going to plant soybeans. Have you heard?

LORNA: *(Sarcastic)* Hot gossip today.

PAM: Shut up.

LORNA: Why soybeans?

PAM: Turns out if you plant the same crop in your fields year after year it sucks the nutrients out of the soil. So you gotta, uh, you gotta change things up so things can grow.

LORNA: ...

PAM: Have you ever thought about doing that?

LORNA: Planting soybeans?

PAM: Or just. You know. Trying a little something new.

LORNA: In my field?

PAM: Yah.

LORNA: But I don't have a field.

PAM: Sure you do.

LORNA: I have a garden.

PAM: I mean metaphorically.

LORNA: Do I want to plant something new in my metaphorical field?

PAM: Yah.

LORNA: Well, no, because it doesn't exist.

PAM: But what if it did?

LORNA: But it doesn't.

PAM: What if the field was you?

LORNA: ???

PAM: What if the field was you and all those years ago you decided you were going to grow corn.

LORNA: But the farmers would have decided that. I'd have just been unthinking dirt.

PAM: Ok then let's say it was me. I was a person, I mean field, and I chose corn. All those years ago I chose corn. And I loved it. And committed to it. And at first, I thought: hey, this is great. Look at all this corn. Who doesn't love corn? But after years and years of supporting the corn and giving the corn what it needs to grow...I feel like the corn has leeched me dry.

LORNA: You the field.

109

PAM: Yes, me the field. The life is sucked out. I'm a husk. And worse: I think I'm starting to rot.

LORNA: Can a husk rot?

PAM: But! But, then one day I see a soybean plant and think, you know, that's different. It smells different. It certainly tastes different. And it's so nice with its kind eyes and big hands.

(Lorna perks up, suddenly getting what they're talking about. She doesn't like it.)

LORNA: The soybean?

PAM: And I start to think, well, maybe this soybean could replenish some of the nutrients I've lost. And maybe the part of me that is rotting could actually be compost that's good for the soybean. It's a mutually beneficial relationship. Win-win.

LORNA: And where did you find this soybean? A bar?

(Pam repositions herself to face away from Lorna.)

PAM: Pretend I didn't say anything.

LORNA: Don't you at least owe it to the corn to make it work?

PAM: This isn't about the corn. It's about my soil.

LORNA: It's about both of them. Without your soil, the corn will die.

PAM: The corn has literally sucked the life out of my soil, making it impossible for it to achieve its full potential.

LORNA: So, should the corn just die?

PAM: No! And it probably won't. It might find another field or learn to be its own field or—

LORNA: You start with soybeans, and next thing you know it's peas, potatoes, horseradish. Lucy Rolfhauser put that horseradish in her garden, and it got everywhere.

PAM: Just because there wouldn't be corn doesn't mean my soil is going to open itself up for every other vegetable in sight. It's just soybeans. And it's probably only for one season.

LORNA: Well, I think corn is just fine, thankyouverymuch.

PAM: Good for you. Enjoy your corn.

LORNA: I will.

PAM: Good.

LORNA: Good.

(Lorna repositions herself.

Then she does it again.

And again.)

You wanna give me another wine cooler?

(Pam hands her a bottle.

Lorna opens it and drinks. A lot. It gives her courage.)

You remember when the foundation of the farmhouse cracked when we were kids, and all those snakes slithered in and made that snake ball in the winter?

PAM: How could I forget? It was the snake ball of '74. They'd come into the basement and we'd find them everywhere. It was like the ground was alive and slithering.

LORNA: And what did mom and dad do? They killed 'em all. One-by-one. Traps, shovels, their bare hands. Then they fixed the foundation. No more snakes in the house. In fact, no more snakes in the yard. Or anywhere in general.

(Genuine question)

Actually, when's the last time you saw a snake?

PAM: What are you saying?

LORNA: Whatever that itch it is you're thinking of scratching, kill it. You don't want snake balls in your basement, and I'm not talking about your house.

(Pam gathers her things in a fury.)

Pam.

PAM: Don't Pam me. Go Pam yourself.

LORNA: Pam.

PAM: I said go Pam yourself.

LORNA: Come on, Pam.

PAM: Pam yourself!!!

(Pam storms off in a fury.)

LORNA: Pam! This is your house!

(Pam stomps back on.)

PAM: Then PAM OFF.
LORNA: Can we talk about—?
PAM: I SAID PAM OFF!

(Lorna takes her things and leaves.

Pam returns to lounging, angry and despondent.

Ted enters.)

TED: Pammy?
PAM: Hey Ted.
TED: Everything alright?
PAM: Mhmm.
TED: Ya sure? I thought I just heard your name a lot.
PAM: ...
TED: Whatcha drinking?
PAM: It's a passion fruit wine cooler. Want one?
TED: I'll stick with beer. What time's dinner?
PAM: 6:00.
TED: Could you make it earlier? I'm gonna play cards with Bruce and the boys.
PAM: Sure.
TED: I won't stay out so late this time if that's what you're gonna say.
PAM: I'm not saying anything.
TED: If that's what you're thinking.
PAM: Stay out as late as you want, Ted. I'll just be right here.

(He leaves.

Sadly, Pam drinks the passion fruit wine cooler.)

SNAKE BALLS IN YOUR BASEMENT

Well, I think it tastes nice.

END OF PLAY

Man Day

WHERE

The Schmidtbauer garage in the very, very, very, very, very small town of Cold Lake, Minnesota. Unfinished projects. Storage. Baseball equipment. A bike. A recycling bin full of uncrushed cans. The final islands of snow on the ground.

WHEN

Spring, 1996. The time of year when any daffodils and tulips that survived the winter are just about to poke out of the ground.

CHARACTERS

BOB – 30s/40s. The type of dad that coaches little league and terrifies the players. A man's man who is probably out of shape.

HUNTER – 7. A gentle boy who's probably more interested in fabrics than athletics.

A NOTE ON THE TEXT

This play is set in rural Minnesota, and as such it's helpful if the characters speak with thick working-class MN accents reminiscent of *Fargo* or *Drop Dead Gorgeous*.

PREMIERE

Man Day was originally performed as part of *From Cold Lake: Episode 1*, which received its world premiere at The Peoples Improv Theater (Ali Reza Farahnakian, Founder and Caretaker; Stephen Stout, Artistic Director) in New York City on August 8th, 2016. The producers were Matt Cox, Kristin McCarthy Parker and Stephen Stout. It was directed by Colin Waitt. Songs and Score were composed by Tommy Crawford. Sound design & mixing was by Matt Cox. The cast was as follows:

HUNTER: Alex Haynes
BOB: Patrick McCartney

Bob and Hunter burst into the garage roaring. It is a little too intense, and they're both having the time of their lives.

BOB & HUNTER: MAN DAY!!! RAAAAAH!

(They take turns roaring at each other, each trying to top the other.

Then:)

BOB: Push-ups!

(The men do push-ups.

Bob gets tired very quickly, but Hunter easily keeps going. Bob, self-conscious, changes the focus.)

Punches!

(They punch at imagined enemies surrounding them.)

BOTH: *(Not in unison)* Pow Pow Pow! Pew Pew Pew! Pow!
BOB: Crush the cans!
HUNTER: Man day!

(They pull cans from the recycling bin and yell "RAH!" every time they crush one.)

BOB: Rah! Suck on that, Waste Management! Rah! Try to fine us for not crushing our cans again! Rah!
HUNTER: Yeah! Rah! Suck it!
BOTH: *(Not in unison)* Rah! Rah! Rah!

(Suddenly, Hunter loses interest and walks back into the house. Bob doesn't notice and continues to crush cans.)

BOB: Rah! Rah! Soup can! That one hurt! Rah!

(Hunter returns with a plastic tube filled with pogs. He calmly sits down and begins to stack them.)

Rah! Rah! Hunter, you want a beer? Rah! ...What are you doing buddy?

HUNTER: I'm playing with pogs.

BOB: What are pogs?

(Hunter makes a big stack of pogs and throws a slammer at them. They fly everywhere.)

BOB: ...That's it?

HUNTER: Uh-huh.

BOB: Where'd you get those?

HUNTER: Mom. See this one? It's Dr. Ellie Sattler from *Jurassic Park*. She's my hero.

BOB: Enough pogs. Let's play some football!

HUNTER: Man day is boring.

BOB: Man day is boring?

HUNTER: Yah.

BOB: *(Hurt, not showing it)* Well ex-ca-use me.

(Bob starts picking up cans. Hunter plays pogs.

A woodpecker begins pecking at the roof. Bob calls put to the bird.)

Hey! Hey! G.D. Woodpecker. I just had that roof re-done!

(Bob throws an empty beer can at the bird, but it falls awkwardly a few feet in front of him.)

HUNTER: It'd work better if it wasn't / open.

BOB: Open. Thanks, brainiac, I know.

(Bob goes to the fridge and gets a full beer. He talks more to himself than anything.)

Give him a tube of pogs and suddenly he thinks he's Alex Trebec.

HUNTER: Alex who?

BOB: Exactly!

(The bird pecking gets louder.)

That's it, fucker, peck on this.

(Bob furiously hurls the unopened can of beer toward the roof. It hits and sprays back onto him. After a small beat, the pecking continues.)

HUNTER: *(Scandalized)* You said the F-H word.
BOB: Sometimes men do that.
HUNTER: Why?
BOB: Because, Hunter, the world is a cruel place.

(Small pause.)

What a waste of beer. I'm gonna get one of my guns.

(Bob starts to walk off.)

HUNTER: Wait!
BOB: ...
HUNTER: ...We could use my slingshot?

(Hunter holds up an impressive slingshot.)

BOB: That's pretty slick. Where'd you get that?
HUNTER: Zach Lange gave it to me for my birthday.
BOB: *(Impressed)* Zach Lange?
HUNTER: Well, mom says it was actually Zach's mom who got it for me because she feels bad that Zach always calls me a gay and beats me up. What's gay?

(Bob grabs the slingshot out of Hunter's hands and does the equivalent of kicking a car's tires: tests how it feels, pulls the rubber, assesses the weight, etc.)

(Re: slingshot) Wanna see?

(Bob nods and hands the slingshot back to Hunter.

Hunter pulls, aims and shoots a rock impressively far.)

See?
BOB: *(Impressed)* Well, what do ya think about that? That's pretty great.

(The pecking starts again.)

Time to show the little bastard who's—

(Bob assertively grabs the slingshot from Hunter's hands.

Hunter holds back tears, interpreting the grab as him not being good enough.

Bob realizes he's hurt Hunter's feelings.)

Hunter, buddy, shake it off.

(Hunter lets out a whimper.

Bob offers an unsure olive branch:)

You think you can hit the bird?
HUNTER: *(No)* Easy.

(Hunter takes his very thick Pure Poison slammer, loads it into his slingshot, and focuses intently on the bird. He lets go, and the slammer glides through the air.

We hear a soft thump.

They watch the unseen bird fall.

THUD.)

BOB: *(To bird, triumphant)* Take that you sonnovabitch!
HUNTER: ...It's not moving. Why isn't it moving?
BOB: I hope it hurt, you stupid fucking—let's not tell mom about the swearing.
HUNTER: Bird? Hey bird?
BOB: Relax, Hunter. You killed him.
HUNTER: What?
BOB: He's dead, Hunter. *(Re: Roof)* Oh buddy, you left / a mark.
HUNTER: Is he coming back?
BOB: Of course not. Once something's dead, it's gone forever. Like grandma when we put her in the ground.
HUNTER: But—

BOB: One day we all die and that's it. *(Re: the roof)* I'm gonna have to paint /
over that.
HUNTER: *(Re: Death)* Really?
BOB: Oh yah. Big lessons on Man Day.

(Small beat.)

I don't know about you, but I want to rip apart some old tires with
my hands. MAN DAY!

(Bob exits.

Hunter stares the bird.)

HUNTER: It's ok. He's gone now. You can wake up.

(Small pause.)

Bird?

(Small pause.)

...Bird?

(Small pause.)

Come back.

(Hunter shivers, suddenly aware of the cold.)

Come back.

(Distraught and guilty, Hunter continues to will the bird back to life.)

END OF PLAY

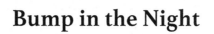

Bump in the Night

WHERE

Reese and Jake's new home in Jefferson City, Missouri.

WHEN

Tonight. Late.

CHARACTERS

REESE – 20s/30s. A singer who relocated for their boyfriend's job. Could be played by an actor of any gender identity.

JAKE – 20s/30s. A supportive man with a sensible office job.

—

Darkness.

Reese and Jake asleep in bed.

Suddenly, Reese wakes up from a nightmare.

Reese screams.

REESE: Aaaah!
JAKE: Oh my God!
REESE: Oh God!
JAKE: Are you alright?
REESE: Yeah, no. I'm sorry.
JAKE: What is happening?!
REESE: Sorry. I'm sorry.
JAKE: Are you hurt?
REESE: Just a dream. Nothing's wrong.

> *(Jake puts his arms around Reese.*
>
> *Reese screams again.)*

Aaaah!
JAKE: It's just me! I'm trying to hug you.
REESE: I'm sorry.
JAKE: Just trying to comfort you.
REESE: I'm sorry.

> *(Jake struggles for a few seconds to find a lamp.*
>
> *He clicks it on.*
>
> *It's not crazy bright and the light reveals a few unpacked moving boxes. Jake is shirtless.*
>
> *They both sit heaving as their eyes adjust. Jake rubs Reese's back gently.)*

Your hands are really soft. Tender.
JAKE: I'll unpack the rest of this tomorrow. I promise.

REESE: ...

JAKE: ...

REESE: That was a night terror. I haven't had one in, God...years?

JAKE: ...This is normal?

REESE: I thought I was better.

(Suddenly embarrassed)

I feel like I'm six and the boogey man is going to get me.

JAKE: Sweetie.

REESE: *(Humiliated)* Sorry.

JAKE: Why didn't you tell me?

REESE: I never had them with you.

JAKE: ...But as, like, a warning?

REESE: Can I touch you?

JAKE: Sure.

REESE: Sorry. I just need a cuddle or.

(They embrace.)

JAKE: ...

REESE: ...

JAKE: Is it 'cause we moved here?

REESE: No.

JAKE: I know Jefferson City doesn't have a ton going on arts-wise, but we'll
     find it.

REESE: I know.

JAKE: We do this for my career now and it sets us up to be able to afford to
     do it for yours later.

REESE: I know, I know.

JAKE: *(Being kind)* You can still sing for me.

REESE: I know you mean well, but it's not the same.

JAKE: ...

REESE: ...

JAKE: I'm sorry.

REESE: No, I'm sorry.

JAKE: ...
REESE: ...
JAKE: ...
REESE: ...
JAKE: Do you want a tea or something?
REESE: Ok.
JAKE: Chamomile? Ginger?
REESE: Which would be more relaxing?
JAKE: Probably the chamomile.
REESE: Perfect.
JAKE: Dumb question, uh. Why isn't your car in the garage?
REESE: It's at the grocery store.
JAKE: ...Why?
REESE: ...
JAKE: ...

(Jake grabs a shirt from the floor and exits to the kitchen.

Reese is alone in the room...and feeling it. Anxious, they pull the blanket around themself and try to slow their breath. This should take a while.

Reese cannot relax and ends up shaking uncontrollably. They get up and busy themself unpacking boxes. They continue to do so until what feels like a reasonable amount of time for Jake to make tea passes.

Jake enters wearing the shirt. He holds two teas. Reese's back is to him.)

JAKE: I can do that tomorrow.
REESE: Sorry, I just thought I'd—
JAKE: Have I ruined your life?
REESE: ...
JAKE: ...

(Reese turns and sees Jake. They gasp.)

What?
REESE: Where did you get that shirt?
JAKE: I grabbed it. It was on the floor.

REESE: No, it wasn't.

JAKE: It was, otherwise how could I have——?

REESE: This isn't funny.

JAKE: Reese.

REESE: ...

JAKE: Reese. This is me.

REESE: ...

JAKE: ...

REESE: Sorry.

(Jake steps toward Reese, but Reese backs up.)

Sorry.

(Jake takes off the shirt and puts on a different one.)

Thank you.

JAKE: What is going on?

REESE: Can I please have the tea?

(They both drink tea.)

JAKE: ...

REESE: ...

JAKE: ...

REESE: I have this, um. I've had these dreams since I was a kid.

JAKE: ...

REESE: They started out of the blue when I was six. My parents thought it was this kind of generalized anxiety about moving to a new town. And the psychiatrist agreed with them. The first one did, at least. We ended up going through five, because no one could get to the bottom of... Eventually they hooked me up to these sleep machines, but they couldn't find anything out of the ordinary. Then again, I never woke up screaming there. Kind of hard to fully relax with all the cables and electrodes. Or maybe he knew they couldn't stop him if they didn't know he was there.

JAKE: ..."He?"

REESE: They were worried I might be a paranoid schizophrenic for a while, but the last two psychiatrists ruled that out, so. I haven't had them since I met you. That's why I haven't said anything. Never felt like I had to. As you can see it's not really a fun, um. It's not a fun conversation to have. And you're probably thinking, "Oh God, what have I gotten myself into?" 'Cause if you're not, you would be the first. I'm such an idiot. I guess I thought you must have fixed me or saved me or...

JAKE: Who is "He?"

REESE: ...

JAKE: ...

REESE: He's the man with no face.

JAKE: Is that from a movie or something?

REESE: No.

JAKE: ...

REESE: ...

JAKE: ...No face?

REESE: It's like the front of his head's been blown off. Pulpy bits of flesh and this dark, um. It's like a mouth. I mean, it is a [mouth]. It's definitely a [mouth]. Sorry, I'm shaking.

JAKE: ...

REESE: I never see it coming. You'd think after all these years, there'd be a pattern, but it's always a surprise. I'm in a dream. Any dream. Then there he is. Out of all the people on earth, it has to be me.

JAKE: Why you?

(Reese puts their hands up: "I don't know.")

REESE: Sometimes I run. Sometimes I can't, because he...

JAKE: ...

REESE: He, uh.

JAKE: ...

REESE: He pulls me close and—it's the same every time but I always experience it as though it's a discovery—his mouth opens wider and wider like a snake or ancient worm. And as his pulpy lips spread, I hear his flesh tearing...like he hasn't eaten in so long he's shrunk from hunger. I try to resist, but I can't. There's no escape. I scream as his lips start at the crown of my head and slide slowly covering my eyes, nose, mouth. I scream as I'm sliced by the teeth in his neck. I keep screaming as I begin to be digested. I scream and scream as my body dissolves, and I become nothing...and then I wake up.

JAKE: You've dreamt this since you were six?

REESE: ...

JAKE: ...

REESE: I think he got out.

JAKE: ...

REESE: ...

JAKE: ...How?

REESE: I don't know, but, um. I saw him. Today. I was at the grocery store, and I grabbed a gallon of milk and I turned, and there he was. Something about him was different. There was a kind of glee. Like the moment had finally arrived. I drop the milk and run. And I just keep running. I avoid everyone, because I'm terrified he could pop out from anywhere. I leave my car thinking maybe he's in the back seat. I run home and I lock all the doors and you're still at work and I'm thinking, "This must be a dream. This has to be a dream." And you text saying your boss is making you stay late. Right?

JAKE: Yeah.

REESE: And I must have fallen asleep waiting because the next thing I know you crawl into bed next to me and I turn to kiss you and you're wearing that shirt and you are him and I scream and you devour me and I'm destroyed and I wake up and it's, what, ten minutes ago?

JAKE: It was all a dream.

REESE: My car's still at the grocery store.

JAKE: Maybe you've mixed last night and your dream together.

REESE: Did you wear that shirt to bed?

JAKE: No, but—

REESE: Did you unpack it?

JAKE: No, it's—

REESE: That's because it's not ours.

JAKE: Sure it is.

REESE: When have either of us worn it?

JAKE: ...

REESE: ...

(Suddenly, a person-like shape moves behind them. We only see it for a moment. Ideally it feels like something we've been looking at this whole time comes to life and then vanishes into the darkness.

Reese and Jake do not see it but sense its presence.)

Are you going to destroy me?

JAKE: Reese, it's me.

REESE: Are you?

(The light goes out. The room is in total darkness.)

JAKE: Reese?

(He moves toward Reese for comfort, but Reese moves away from him.)

REESE: Don't.

JAKE: I'm still / me.

REESE: Stay away from me.

JAKE: But I'm / not.

REESE: STOP!

JAKE: *(Desperate)* Reese, please!

REESE: I SAID STAY AWAY.

(Reese violently shoves Jake away.)

JAKE: I'm really scared. Please don't make me stay over here.

REESE: ...

JAKE: ...

REESE: ...

JAKE: ...

REESE: ...

JAKE: ...

(Reese senses that Jake is gone.)

REESE: I know you're there. It's been you all along. Say something. SAY SOMETHING.

(In blackness, Reese fumbles in their pocket and finds their phone. They turn on the flashlight and shines it toward where Jake was standing.

Nothing is there.

Reese gasps and accidentally drops the phone. It lands in such a way that it reveals Jake [or is it Jake?] behind Reese. He is wearing the shirt from the dream. Reese does not know he's there.

Reese picks up the phone and does a slow 360-degree scan of the room. When the light reaches the place where Jake stood [or was it Jake?], nothing is there.)

...Jake?

(Suddenly, a hand reaches out from under the bed and grabs Reese's leg. It pulls.

Reese struggles against something we cannot see that slowly pulls them head-first under the bed. Flesh rips. A slurp. Reese screams until unseen lips pass over their head.

With muffled cries, Reese puts up a good fight...but it is a losing battle. Whatever is pulling slowly devours them.

Eventually, Reese's legs stop moving and—lifeless—the are dragged under the bed.

We linger on the still stage for a few moments until:

Blackout.)

END OF PLAY

Hello Again

WHERE

The New York City subway. Specifically, on the L train headed from Manhattan to Brooklyn.

WHEN

This afternoon.

CHARACTERS

BRITTANY – Late 20s. The one who was popular.
RACHEL – Late 20s. The one who was not.

Rachel and Brittany board the L train separately. Rachel sits and reads a motivational self-help book in the vein of The Secret or Uncover Your Potential.

Brittany considers her for a few moments, toying with her necklace. She approaches.

BRITTANY: Rachel Wallace?

RACHEL: Um. Yes?

BRITTANY: Brittany Stevens. We went to high school together.

RACHEL: Oh wow. Hi!

BRITTANY: Hi!

(They hug.)

RACHEL: Look at you! You look exactly the same.

BRITTANY: Stop.

RACHEL: Seriously, you look amazing. How are you?!

BRITTANY: I'm great! Wow. I've been staring at you for like ten minutes trying to figure out is that Rachel? Is it not Rachel?

RACHEL: It is.

BRITTANY: Yeah. Wow. You live in New York now?

RACHEL: I do. I'm, uh, on my way home from work, actually.

BRITTANY: Really? What do you do?

RACHEL: Uh. Well. I have three jobs. Today I was walking people's dogs in Chelsea.

BRITTANY: Cute.

RACHEL: Then a couple of days a week I take reservations for a restaurant. And then every so often I get these gigs where I pretend I'm a patient for medical students and they have to figure out what's wrong with me.

BRITTANY: Wow.

RACHEL: Yeah. Some days it's cancer, some days it's chlamydia. Not exactly my dream, but it pays the bills.

BRITTANY: You gotta eat.

RACHEL: Exactly. What about you?

BRITTANY: I work in TV.

RACHEL: Oh.

BRITTANY: I was at HBO, but now I'm at Netflix.

RACHEL: Have you worked on anything I would have seen?

BRITTANY: Yeah.

(Small pause.)

You ruined my life.

RACHEL: ...What?

BRITTANY: You ruined my life, and here we are.

RACHEL: ...

BRITTANY: ...

RACHEL: Welp, this is my stop.

BRITTANY: Oh weird.

RACHEL: Naw, First Ave is really nice.

BRITTANY: I could have sworn you lived in Brooklyn. The DeKalb stop?

RACHEL: ...Excuse me?

BRITTANY: In the railroad building with the kind of greenish roof?

RACHEL: ...

BRITTANY: Ok, so I lied. I've had my eye on you for more than ten
minutes.

RACHEL: ...

BRITTANY: ...

RACHEL: ...Do you want something?

BRITTANY: ...

RACHEL: ...

BRITTANY: ...

RACHEL: I'm going to go to the other side of the car.

BRITTANY: Who took the photos you posted of me?

RACHEL: ...

BRITTANY: You know what I'm talking about.

RACHEL: ...

BRITTANY: Were you the one who took them?

RACHEL: ...

BRITTANY: I was sixteen. Did you take the naked photos of me?

RACHEL: What do you want?

BRITTANY: I want to know who took the photos you posted.

RACHEL: ...

BRITTANY: My mom told me your dad is sick. I'm sorry. I'd like to set you free.

RACHEL: ...What?

BRITTANY: Haven't you ever wondered why *nothing* seems to work out for you?

(Brittany smiles.)

Friends, jobs, boyfriends. What could possibly keep going wrong? Nice book, by the way.

RACHEL: ...

BRITTANY: My therapist has been trying to get me to open myself up to the idea that I shouldn't focus all my anger on you. She says it's not helpful. She's been saying that for years. "It's not helpful." I mean, enough with the broken record, lady! Right?! But then the other day she said, "You know, Brittany, since you've brought up the photos again, I have to ask: is there anything that might help open the door that would allow you to begin to move on?" I mean, can you imagine? What kind of insensitive person says this to someone? Then she said, "Brittany, let's acknowledge again that what happened was awful. But! Might it be helpful to think about what could have compelled Rachel to do this in the first place?" And I was like, "Are you asking me to feel sympathy for the person who posted naked photos of me as a minor without my consent?" And she said, "No, of course not. But! Would it help you to move on if you explored some of the circumstances that might cause an adolescent to do something without thinking of the painful consequences?" And I was like, "Are you asking me to justify my trauma?" And she said, "No. But! I'm asking you to consider that things may be more complicated than they feel. For example, is it possible she may have experienced trauma of her own?" And I said no, because you hadn't, right?

RACHEL: ...

BRITTANY: Have you? You can tell me. Honestly, maybe it'll change things. I don't know.

RACHEL: ...

BRITTANY: I'm gonna take that as a no. So, I was right. Therapists, man. And then she said, "Well, have you ever considered that Rachel may not have acted alone?" And that gave me pause. I'd spent all these years focused on you. You the monster. You the criminal. I had never considered that other people could be involved. So, I left the session I guess open to entertaining the idea that it wasn't just you. But if there's someone else out there, how could this possibly help me move on? That I couldn't reconcile. But then I heard about your dad. Stage four, right?

RACHEL: ...

BRITTANY: Oh, did I mumble that?

(A touch too loud)

Stage four, right?

RACHEL: Yes.

BRITTANY: It's like the universe finally gets it. It's like there actually is justice out there, and it's not all on me to make you pay. So, now that the universe has caught up, it feels like I can finally move on. You have had such an outsized power in my life for so long, it's time to set us both free. But before that can happen, I need to know...did someone else take the photos?

RACHEL: I know you may not believe it, but this has haunted me since high school.

BRITTANY: It's haunted *you*?!

RACHEL: Were you the one who called the parents of the children I'd been nannying and told them you saw me touch [them], uh?

BRITTANY: ...

RACHEL: That is on my record. It is something I did not do.

BRITTANY: ...

RACHEL: I'm going to be sick.

BRITTANY: ...

RACHEL: I've spent the past ten years trying to atone for what I did. I've volunteered for everything. I've raised money, marched, made calls. On top of struggling to stay afloat because I haven't been able to keep a job. And I kept pushing. I kept pushing because I thought if I pushed hard enough, I could be worthy of being alive.

BRITTANY: ...

RACHEL: Was the Tarrell thing you?

BRITTANY: ...

RACHEL: We were going to [get married].

BRITTANY: ...

RACHEL: It's been a decade. Why can't you [move on]?

BRITTANY: You put naked photos of me online.

RACHEL: I was seventeen. I was an idiot. I wouldn't do that now.

BRITTANY: Not "I'm sorry?"

RACHEL: You've actually ruined my life.

BRITTANY: They're still out there. No matter how many times I've had them removed. It's like people keep making copies. With my name. And everyone always finds them. They always do. Kind of hard to be the boss when people forward each other naked pictures of you as a teenager. Everyone I go out with...eventually we have to have the same conversation if they haven't already looked me up online before our first date. My favorite is the strangers who reach out to tell me in detail what they're going to do to my sixteen-year-old body. What did I even do to you?

RACHEL: I wish I could undo it. I was a teenager and stupid and...you were good at everything, and it wasn't fair. I know that's ridiculous to think about now. But at the time it was everything.

BRITTANY: Did I do anything to hurt you?

RACHEL: Why wouldn't you let me in?

BRITTANY: ...

RACHEL: You were popular. The soccer captain. Homecoming Queen. Everyone wanted to be you. Why wouldn't you share even a little of it?

BRITTANY: ...

RACHEL: But hey: you landed on your feet. People like you always do. It doesn't matter anymore. So let it go. You need to let it go.

BRITTANY: ...

RACHEL: ...

BRITTANY: Ten years. How is that even possible?

RACHEL: ...

BRITTANY: ...

RACHEL: ...

BRITTANY: Are you going home for the reunion?

RACHEL: Haven't decided yet. You?

BRITTANY: I'm gonna skip it.

RACHEL: Fair.

BRITTANY: I am actually sorry about your dad.

RACHEL: Thanks.

BRITTANY: ...

RACHEL: ...

BRITTANY: ...

RACHEL: There was someone else.

BRITTANY: ...

RACHEL: I got him to crawl up that tree outside your parents' bathroom, and. He was the one who sent them to me.

BRITTANY: Who was it?

RACHEL: Will you actually leave me alone?

BRITTANY: Yes.

RACHEL: How do I know you're telling the truth?

BRITTANY: You can trust me.

RACHEL: ...

BRITTANY: Fine. I can keep doing what I've been—

RACHEL: It was Justin Posner.

BRITTANY: ...Who's Justin Posner?

RACHEL: Exactly. We were nobodies.

BRITTANY: Are you pulling that name out of the air?

RACHEL: He's a real person.

(Brittany stares at Rachel, trying to decide if she's telling the truth.

Then:)

BRITTANY: This is my stop. Nice bumping into you.

(She pulls out her phone and plays part of a freshly recorded voice memo.)

RACHEL: *(A recording)* "It doesn't matter anymore. So let it go. You need to let it go."

(Rachel tries to grab the phone, Brittany pulls it away.)

BRITTANY: The Internet will have fun with that. Thanks for the tip about Justin.

(Rachel lunges for the phone.)

Help! She's attacking me!

(Rachel backs off, suddenly aware of everyone else on the train.)

Smile.

(She gestures to a tiny camera in her necklace.)

You're on Candid Camera. Find me in ten years. Tell me how much this doesn't matter.

(She exits the train.

Rachel begins to shake. Her phone pings. And again. And again. It pings relentlessly. She looks at it.)

RACHEL: Oh my God. She posted my number.

END OF PLAY

Shift Swap

WHERE

A mid-range restaurant in New York City.

WHEN

Today.

CHARACTERS

LAURA – 20s. What one might call an ingenue.

VAL – 20s/30s. What one might call a character actor.

Laura and Val during the transition from lunch to dinner.

Laura finishes tying her apron.

LAURA: What are you giving me?

VAL: Ten, twelve, fifteen. Drinks, entrees, dessert.

LAURA: Just drop their check.

VAL: I would if I didn't hate them. Bye!

LAURA: Question: what are you doing Tuesday?

VAL: I'm not taking your shift.

LAURA: Just wanted to float it by you...

VAL: Hard no.

LAURA: Would you cover my lunch? I'd let you borrow one of my wigs.

VAL: Ask Eddie.

LAURA: I already did. PLEASE?! I got a huge audition! Ok, maybe not
      huge. I got AN audition.

VAL: Pass the napkins.

LAURA: Here, I'll do them for you. So—

VAL: I'm gonna refill the—

LAURA: I'll do all of your side work. I don't mind. It reminds me of the
      time I played a waitress in a play instead of, you know, was one.

VAL: ...

LAURA: Look, I submit my stuff every day. There are ten trillion women in
      this city that look just like me. Most of them in Equity. With
      agents. And connections. They're prettier. Or more "real" looking.
      Or more "characterful." Please don't make me say no to a yes.

VAL: Table twelve needs you.

LAURA: COMING!

(*Laura runs off. Val rolls silverware. She's done it so many times she could do
it in her sleep.*

After a moment, Laura runs on.)

Are there eggs in the aioli?

VAL: It's mayonnaise.

LAURA: ...So?

VAL: Yes.

LAURA: *(Running back to the floor)* I WAS WRONG! DON'T EAT IT!

(Laura returns.)

Anyway, totally no rush, no pressure...but I really need to know by—

VAL: Is it at least a good part?

LAURA: Uh, well, they're looking for an actress who's quirky but not weird, grounded but not dull, beautiful but doesn't know it, intelligent, fierce, but still likeable. Like, there's nothing wrong with her, but she still has a lot going on inside. Does that sound like me? Or any human woman? Anyway, it's not written yet. It's going to be devised.

VAL: Ask Juan.

LAURA: They'll build it around me. Plus, it's aiming high, which is more than you can say about most plays today. What is it you're always saying about everything you see?

VAL: It makes me understand why people don't go to the theater.

LAURA: Exactly! And this, it won't be like that! It's going to be about real things. Race. Gender. Sexuality. The Constitution. Colonialism. Social Media. Polarization. Donald Trump. Ok, so maybe it's trying to do a lot but. I'd give you comps?

VAL: Is it at least paid?

LAURA: ...

VAL: Laura.

LAURA: Please. I need this.

VAL: Call Keesha.

LAURA: I could give you a free voice lesson.

VAL: I'm busy.

LAURA: Please.

VAL: I'm not going to rearrange my life so you can be exploited in a show no one will see.

LAURA: I'm paying my dues.

VAL: To who?

LAURA: Look, just because you've given up on acting doesn't mean I can't still try.

VAL: ...

LAURA: Sorry. That was.

VAL: ...

LAURA: Sorry.

VAL: ...

LAURA: Um. I know this is a bad time to ask, but. Is there egg in the chicken sandwich?

VAL: ...

LAURA: *(Running off)* DON'T EAT THE CHICKEN!

(Val continues to roll silverware, both hurt and angry.

Laura returns.)

VAL: ...

LAURA: ...

VAL: So, when you were at Julliard—

LAURA: I didn't go to / Julliard.

VAL: Sorry, when you were at Yale.

LAURA: You know I didn't—

VAL: It's not going to happen.

LAURA: ...

VAL: I know that's hard to hear, but take it from someone who's been told since she was fifteen that she'll be really castable once she's over forty. 'Cause I guess I don't look like what people would believe could be a real person yet. Only they're not going to hire me when I'm older, 'cause I have no resume. They're going to hire someone who's been working since she looked like you. But it won't be you, 'cause you have never worked. 'Cause you didn't go somewhere fancy. Or have famous parents. Or sleep with someone. Or lightning didn't strike. This unpaid play no one's going to see— would you even watch it if you weren't in it?

LAURA: ...

VAL: Exactly. It's not going to happen. It's better you wrap your head around that now than spend the rest of your life poor and wondering why you've never been enough.

LAURA: I work.

VAL: Waiting tables.

LAURA: ...

VAL: Your fans need you.

LAURA: *(To unseen table 12)* GIVE ME LIKE TWO SECONDS.

(To Val)

And who are you? All you need is a cigarette and a martini and you're straight out of central casting for "Sad, Pithy Theater Woman Who's So Jaded She's Basically a Drag Queen." You're not exactly an expert.

(Val gets up to leave.)

VAL: Best of luck covering your shift.

LAURA: I'm sorry.

VAL: He's really going to town on that egg custard.

LAURA: *(Running to unseen table 12)* DO NOT EAT THE CUSTARD! THE CUSTARD HAS EGGS!

(After a moment, Laura returns.)

Turns out it's just a preference, not an allergy.

VAL: I hate people.

LAURA: ...

VAL: ...

LAURA: So, we're not in anything. Who cares? Ok, I care. My God, I care. I care so much I could just rip off my clothes and—

VAL: Don't.

LAURA: One time I played this woman who lost her baby and it's just like that. "WHY ME, GOD?! MY BABY!"

VAL: Stop.

LAURA: We have to try. We just have to. These are our lives, dammit! I would sell my plasma or my eggs or, honestly at this point I'd be willing to sell my soul just to have my life not be seven twelve-hour days each week of working, running around, begging someone to cover my shifts. I would sell my soul. And maybe Satan would be like, YOUR DREAMS WILL NOT COME TRUE IN THIS WORLD, BUT I'LL ALLOW THEM TO HAPPEN IN AN ALTERNATE UNIVERSE. And honestly, at this point, I'd say, yeah, that's enough for me.

VAL: Selling your soul and it still only happens in an alternate reality?

LAURA: Yeah. Maybe that's the best I can hope for. But there I'd be: on actual Broadway. Or, hell, I'd settle for one of those rehearsal rooms in Midtown. You know, one of those small ones? Where it's like, you're charging how much for the privilege of being in this box?!

VAL: I hate this industry.

LAURA: Even if it's only in some parallel universe: there we are. Not wondering who those other people are who actually made it happen. Or how they did it. Those people are us. The hustle paid off. We are two actors acting. We are enough.

VAL: You're very green.

LAURA: Green things grow.

VAL: Sometimes.

LAURA: ...

VAL: ...

LAURA: Anyway. See you when I see you.

> *(Laura adjusts something sadly and walks toward the dining room. It's not performative. She's genuinely disappointed this won't work out.*
>
> *Just as she's almost gone:)*

VAL: What are you doing Sunday?

LAURA: ...You want to hang out with me?

VAL: I could use some cover for my Sunday brunch.

LAURA: Oh.

VAL: Uh-huh.

LAURA: But brunch is like the opening scene from *Saving Private Ryan*.

VAL: Do you want me to cover your Tuesday or what?

LAURA: BruchIsGreatThankYouILoveYou!

> *(Laura hugs Val.*
>
> *Laura pulls out her phone and presses a few buttons.)*

I initiated the swap in Scheduler, so it's yours whenever you—

VAL: I'll do it when I get home.

LAURA: Please, we've come so far!

(Reluctantly, Val takes out her phone and confirms the shift swap. Laura dances with joy.)

VAL: No phones on the floor.

LAURA: I owe you.

VAL: I take whisky, cash.

LAURA: Well, lucky you, because I once played a stripper who—

VAL: Be careful, Laura. This city is hard enough. Don't let the theater snobs chew you up.

LAURA: You know Keesha told me you were really good in that show at— was it The Brick? The Flea?

VAL: That was, like, three years ago. It was The Tank.

LAURA: She said it was the longest four hours of her life, but you were very moving. And you know Keesha. She hates everything.

VAL: Yes, that is why we're friends.

LAURA: Just to put it out there: if you ever decide to audition again or take a vacation or, you know, you go to a job interview for literally anywhere else even if it's not your dream but it's just something that you think might make you feel like you are more than someone people lie to about their dietary restrictions...

VAL: ...You want to take the rest of my brunches?

LAURA: Why are you still at work?! You're in New York! See a show! Go to a museum!

VAL: I left you the rest of my side work.

LAURA: ...Ok.

VAL: Break a leg.

LAURA: Thanks.

VAL: But for real. Blow 'em away.

LAURA: I'll try.

(Val exits as Laura is waved down by the unseen table 12.)

Oh, it's actually an egg allergy?! Stay calm! I have an epipen from the time I played a nurse! TRY NOT TO PANIC!

END OF PLAY

Cat Call

Outside a trendy restaurant in Manhattan's Flatiron District; inside a car in Central Minnesota.

WHEN
Today. Early evening in NYC, late afternoon in MN.

CHARACTERS
SAM – 20s/30s. A pre-emerging writer who works full-time as a server. Could be played by an actor of any gender identity.

RHONDA – Late 60s. Sam's mom. An alcoholic who talks at, not with.

A NOTE ON THE TEXT
It's helpful if what Sam is leaving unspoken is that they do not actually have a meeting with The Public and Luis has ended their relationship. Rhonda should believe The Public meeting is real and not realize Sam is actually at work.

Sam enters pulling out a pack of cigarettes. They're dressed in server attire, perhaps with an apron.

SAM: *(To unseen co-worker)* Everyone's on dessert. I promise I'll be quick. Just ten minutes. Please? Look, I'll even set an alarm.

(Sam sets an alarm on their phone.

They put a cigarette to their lips and flick a lighter.

Their phone rings. They reject the call.

It rings again. They let it go to voicemail.

It rings a third time. They answer. Maybe we see Rhonda, maybe she's on a microphone in the tech booth.

Rhonda periodically sips something, which Sam can hear her do over the phone.)

SAM: Hi, mom.

RHONDA: Hi, sweetie. I hope I'm not interrupting.

SAM: No, / it's.

RHONDA: I was sitting on the couch and you kind of popped into my head. You know my couch. The one with the flowers?

SAM: You have one couch.

RHONDA: How's Luis?

SAM: ...

RHONDA: Anyway, I was looking at the flowers thinking how they look so good. Really nice roses and, uh, well, I don't really know what the other kind is. Something light yellow. But I thought it might be nice to maybe plant the same flowers in the yard, so—

SAM: I can't really talk. I have a meeting.

RHONDA: That's exciting! What's it for?

SAM: Uh. They might do one of my plays at The Public.

RHONDA: Oh wow! Is that a big deal?

SAM: It would be to me.

RHONDA: Well, fingers crossed! Sure beats the restaurant, right?

SAM: Yeah.

RHONDA: It was so sad seeing you working there. What a waste of your talents. What was I talking about? Oh yeah, my flower couch. It looks so good with the nice roses and the, well, I don't really know what the other—

SAM: Have you been drinking?

RHONDA: No.

SAM: Mom.

RHONDA: I was on my couch, / and.

SAM: I hear liquid.

RHONDA: It's just water. What about you? Are you smoking?

SAM: No.

RHONDA: Are you lying to your mother?

SAM: No.

RHONDA: Great. Then we're both telling the truth and can trust each other.

SAM: ...

RHONDA: So, I'm sitting here on my flower couch, / and.

SAM: Goodbye, mom.

RHONDA: You kind of popped into my head, and.

(Rhonda sobs.)

SAM: ...

RHONDA: ...

SAM: ...

RHONDA: ...

SAM: I think you should get some water.

RHONDA: *(Sobs)* The cat's sick.

SAM: ...

RHONDA: She threw up on my, on my couch. You know, the one with the flowers?

SAM: ...

RHONDA: ...

SAM: ...Have you cleaned it, / or?

RHONDA: *(Sobs)* She won't stop. Everything that goes in comes right out. She's like a squirt gun. I think she's dying!

SAM: ...

RHONDA: I'm at the vet.

SAM: You drove?!

RHONDA: They told me I should put her down and I came back to my car and I. I.

SAM: Mom.

RHONDA: I can't.

SAM: Mom.

RHONDA: Help me.

SAM: Call a cab.

RHONDA: Please help me.

SAM: Fine, what's the address? I'll call / one.

RHONDA: Help me do the right thing.

SAM: ...

RHONDA: ...

SAM: Is she really that bad?

RHONDA: I've been laying newspapers out, because I think she's forgotten where the litter box is. Not like she has much to push out. I think she's forgotten where the food bowl is too. Or that's she's supposed to eat.

SAM: Oh Midnight.

RHONDA: So, now she's puking on the couch, and I don't know how much more I can take. She's part of the family. But she's a burden. But I don't want to hurt her. But.

SAM: ...

RHONDA: Remember when she was a kitten?

SAM: ...

RHONDA: I didn't want another pet, not after Daisy got run over. Oh Daisy...

(Rhonda cries.)

SAM: Please go inside and get some water.

RHONDA: I have water.

SAM: Please focus.

RHONDA: I didn't want to replace Daisy. But Uncle Jim, who should have got his cat fixed really, brought her 'round. Talk about not giving me a choice. Said she was his favorite of the litter. Wanted her to go to someone special. Then you keep her, Jim! But I knew you wanted a pet.

SAM: Mom.

RHONDA: When you left, you broke her heart.

SAM: That's not fair.

RHONDA: What else could she do but fall apart?

SAM: ...

RHONDA: ...

SAM: ...

RHONDA: ...

SAM: ...

RHONDA: ...

SAM: ...

RHONDA: ...

SAM: I think you should take her back inside.

RHONDA: I can't.

SAM: It's the right thing to do.

RHONDA: But it's her life.

SAM: Mom.

RHONDA: Help me.

SAM: If you're not going to do it, why did you call me?

RHONDA: Please don't do this to me when I'm old.

SAM: I'm not going to euthanize you.

RHONDA: Please don't take it all away.

SAM: ...

RHONDA: ...

SAM: I'm going to call the police and ask them to send someone to drive you home.

RHONDA: Sam.

SAM: What's the name of the vet?

RHONDA: I'm not drunk.

SAM: Ok. I'll see if they can run your plates, and—

RHONDA: Fine. I'm taking her inside.

SAM: Mom.

RHONDA: That's what you want. That's what you want, isn't it?

SAM: Mom.

RHONDA: Isn't this what you want?

SAM: ...

RHONDA: ...

SAM: ...

RHONDA: ...

SAM: Can I say goodbye?

RHONDA: Sure. Here she is. She's being quiet. Poor Midnight. I think she knows.

SAM: Bye, Midnight.

RHONDA: Oh God, she's shaking.

SAM: Hold her tight. Hold her tight for me. Oh, Midnight, I'm sorry. I'm so sorry.

(Small pause.)

RHONDA: Would you say a prayer?

SAM: I don't really, uh.

RHONDA: Just in case.

SAM: Why don't you do it?

RHONDA: You're better with words.

SAM: ...

RHONDA: ...

SAM: ...

RHONDA: ...

SAM: God, if you are out there...

RHONDA: ...

SAM: Please release Midnight from her pain.

RHONDA: ...

SAM: ...

RHONDA: ...

SAM: May we all be released from our pain.

RHONDA: ...

SAM: ...

RHONDA: ...

SAM: ...

(They linger in the silence until Sam's phone alarm goes off [*See note at end of play].)

SAM: Shit. I have to get back to work.

RHONDA: I hope the meeting goes well.

SAM: What?

RHONDA: Your meeting. About your play.

SAM: I'm sorry about the cat. Love you.

RHONDA: Love you more.

SAM: Goodbye, Midnight.

RHONDA: Call me.

SAM: Please don't drive.

RHONDA: My poor couch.

SAM: Please don't—

(She hangs up.

Sam stands, distraught. They look at the cigarette they never smoked.

Finally, they return to work.)

END OF PLAY

*NOTE

I know what you're thinking...the build up to that silence has to happen in exactly ten minutes? Really?!

It's less important that it takes exactly ten minutes for the actors to play the scene until the alarm goes off than it is that the alarm goes off in the silence of Sam and Rhonda praying to be released from their pain. Sam will always say it's ten minutes, but you should feel out a timer setting that generally syncs up to the rhythm you find in rehearsal. Maybe it's 9:37, maybe it's 10:52. The audience will never know the difference, and the actors can linger in that active silence for a long while.

Botticelli

WHERE

A bench near a quiet, gator-filled lake in swampland Florida.

WHEN

Sunset. Today.

CHARACTERS

SILK – 30s/40s. A professional assassin. Well dressed, smart, doesn't suffer
fools. An excellent poker face. More of a leader.

HAPPY – 20s/30s. A professional assassin. Not the brightest crayon in the
box. More of a follower.

A NOTE ON THE TEXT

Both characters can be played by actors of any gender identity. Silk should
always talk about being a good mom to Happy, even if the actor playing
them does not identify as female.

Silk and Happy, two assassins, pretend to bird watch.

Happy wears clothes that are appropriate for swampland Florida. Shorts. Perhaps a Hawaiian shirt.

Silk is overdressed in all black. Perhaps they wear a long, stylish coat. They are agitated to have to be here.

One or both of them has binoculars.

HAPPY: Are you the president?
SILK: No, I am not Joe Biden.
HAPPY: Are you America's Next Top Model?
SILK: No, I am not Tyra Banks.
HAPPY: *(Spotting something)* Oh look! It's a, what is it?

(*Happy pulls out a book like <u>Birds of Florida</u> and pages through.*)

Looks kind of like a crow.
SILK: It's a crow.
HAPPY: I think it might be a crow.
SILK: It's a crow.
HAPPY: Someone's testy.
SILK: Let's play a game where you don't talk.
HAPPY: Who pissed in your cornflakes?
SILK: Starting now.

(*They survey silently for a beat or two. It is sooooo hard for Happy to not talk.*

Then:)

HAPPY: Are you a singer who seems like he has fifty Christmas albums, but I think it's actually just the one?
SILK: No, I am not Michael Bublé.
HAPPY: THIS IS SO HARD!
SILK: Don't blow our cover, you dipshit!
HAPPY: Chill out, I'm just a bird watcher. Look at me watching birds. Oh, that one is—that one is definitely getting eaten by a snake.

(They watch the unseen snake devour the bird.)

Wow. Florida is so…Florida. We came here once when I was a kid. This lady was walking her dog and a gator leapt out from some brush and just. Ate it. Then it went for the lady. I would have helped, but I was six. So, I just—

(Silk stomps hard on Happy's foot. Happy recoils in pain.)

Ouch! I wasn't even doing anything!
SILK: Focus.
HAPPY: Ok. Ow. Ow.
SILK: ...
HAPPY: ...
SILK: ...
HAPPY: Is your love on top?
SILK: No, I am not Beyoncé.

(Happy swats a mosquito.)

HAPPY: Why did it have to be Florida?
SILK: Madame Wu said don't ask questions.
HAPPY: But Florida?
SILK: ...
HAPPY: Least she could have done was sent us to a beach.
SILK: This is a beach.
HAPPY: An ocean beach, not a swamp.
SILK: It's a lake.
HAPPY: It's a swamp.

(Silk grabs Happy by the throat.)

SILK: I didn't come here to discuss the nuance of aquatic shorelines. It's a lake or I break your fucking teeth.

(Silk releases Happy.)

HAPPY: You got anger issues. You should see someone about that.
SILK: Coming from someone who dismembers old ladies.

HAPPY: Only the ones who have it coming. And it's not anger. I'm just good with a saw.

(Happy spots a bird and consults the book.)

Now, that. That is an interesting looking bird. What do you suppose it—?

SILK: It's another crow.

HAPPY: You sure? It's got really red legs—

SILK: They're all fucking crows.

HAPPY: ...

SILK: ...

HAPPY: Is your friend Bevis?

SILK: No, I am not Butthead.

HAPPY: Do you play a soprano sax?

SILK: ...

HAPPY: ...

SILK: I think you're confusing Kenny G and Michael Bolton, but no.

HAPPY: No, you're not?

SILK: I'm not either of them.

HAPPY: Are you a single lady?

SILK: Still not Beyoncé.

HAPPY: *(Waving)* Hello, gator.

SILK: Don't provoke it.

HAPPY: I'm just looking.

SILK: You're attracting it with your hand.

HAPPY: It's not like I'm throwing it ham.

SILK: You should respect nature.

HAPPY: Calm down, Mom.

SILK: Trust me, if I was your mom, things would have turned out much differently.

HAPPY: My mom didn't strangle people with barbed wire.

SILK: That you know of.

HAPPY: My mom was a good person.

(Suddenly feeling very defensive, Silk slams Happy's head onto the bench. Happy nearly falls to the ground.)

SILK: *(Sensitive)* I'm a good person.
HAPPY: You nutjob! You're the one that's gonna get us caught!

(Silk winds up to slam Happy's head again.)

SILK: And I'd've been a good parent. You'd've been lucky to be my kid.
HAPPY: *(Breathless)* Ok, I give up! I give up! You'd have been a great parent. Everyone should send you their kids.

(Silk releases Happy.

Silk checks the time as Happy moves as far away from Silk as possible on the bench.)

SILK: Should be here any minute now.
HAPPY: ...
SILK: ...
HAPPY: ...
SILK: ...
HAPPY: You that actress?
SILK: No, I'm not Sandra Bullock.
HAPPY: The one with the face?
SILK: No, I'm not Cate Blanchett.
HAPPY: The dead one with the face.
SILK: I'm not Ingrid Bergman.
HAPPY: Face and the voice.
SILK: I'm not Lauren Bacall.
HAPPY: But funny.
SILK: I'm not Lucille Ball.
HAPPY: Are you Beyoncé?
SILK: Enough with Beyoncé!

(Happy pulls out some trail mix and begins to munch.)

HAPPY: What's it like, killing a kid?
SILK: ...What?
HAPPY: This is the bench where you did it, right?
SILK: ...

HAPPY: Are you ignoring me?

SILK: ...

HAPPY: Are you?

SILK: ...

HAPPY: Fine. Don't answer. Madame Wu told me.

SILK: ...

HAPPY: What was it like? Was it fun?

SILK: Put that crap away. You're attracting the crows.

HAPPY: *(Putting the snack away)* How long did it take her to realize what was happening?

SILK: Drop it or I shoot you.

HAPPY: Calm down.

SILK: *(Deadly)* I said drop it.

HAPPY: ...

SILK: ...

HAPPY: ...

SILK: ...

HAPPY: Are you the shark from *Jaws*?

SILK: ...

HAPPY: ...

SILK: No.

HAPPY: No, you are not...

SILK: It doesn't have a name.

HAPPY: It does. They called it something on set.

SILK: How am I supposed to know that?

HAPPY: It's called the Internet.

SILK: This isn't fair.

HAPPY: It starts with a B. I'm not breaking any rules.

SILK: No, I am not B shark. Bull shark. Whatever it's called. Shark that starts with B.

HAPPY: Bruce.

SILK: What?

HAPPY: Its name was Bruce. See for yourself.

(Silk pulls out their phone and looks up the name of the shark.

While they do, Happy spots a gator.)

Sneaky buggers, aren't they? This one's eyes just slid up over the water. I think he's been watching us this whole time.
SILK: *(On phone)* You're right. They called it Bruce.
HAPPY: Are you dead or alive?
SILK: It has to be a yes or no question.
HAPPY: Are you dead?
SILK: Yes, I'm dead.
HAPPY: Good answer.

(Happy whips out a piece of wire and strangles Silk.

Silk struggles but is unable to overpower Happy.)

You really should have killed that kid.
SILK: *(Choking)* You don't have to do this.
HAPPY: Nah. Not smart to piss off Madame Wu, don't you think?

(Silk struggles and thrashes, unable to free themself.)

I do have one question, though. If you're not Beyoncé, who are you?

(Silk tries to talk but can't.)

What? Oh shit— is this better?

(Happy slightly loosens the wire. Silk gulps in air.)

SILK: *(Wheezing)* I'll tell you if you don't kill me.
HAPPY: That's not fair.

(Silk pulls the wire super tight and strangles themself with all their might. Happy freaks out.)

Fine! Fine! Tell me and I'll let you go.
SILK: *(Wheezing)* I don't trust you.
HAPPY: Good. I don't trust you.
SILK: ...

HAPPY: ...

(Silk releases the wire and breathes heavily for a beat or two.

Then:)

SILK: I'm Botticelli.
HAPPY: Botti-who-i?
SILK: Botticelli. The person this game is named after.
HAPPY: ???
SILK: Renaissance painter. Birth of Venus.
HAPPY: THAT's what this game is called?
SILK: Yeah.
HAPPY: Who the hell even knows that?
SILK: Everyone.
HAPPY: No, they don't.
SILK: Really?
HAPPY: No! Now I don't feel bad for doing this.

(Happy tightens the wire and strangles Silk.)

You pretentious fuck And just so you know: Madame Wu figured out where the girl is. So, as soon as Mr. Gator there has his way with you, I'm gonna pay her a visit.
SILK: *(Choking)* There are limits! We must have limits!
HAPPY: As my mother used to say, sometimes you just gotta fucking do your job.

(Happy tightens the wire. Silk begins to die.)

Great woman, my mother. They really broke the mold.

(Happy spots a bird, and—while still choking Silk—pulls out the bird book and thumbs to a page.)

Ah right! There's another one. I'd have thought crow too, except for the pulsing red legs. Oh! Now I get it. It's a crow being devoured by fire ants. Oh man. Florida.

(Silk dies.

Happy stands for a few moments, suddenly sad.

They adjust Silk's hair or part of their clothing—perhaps a collar? It's done tenderly and with great respect.)

You were one of the good ones.

(Small pause.)

Who's hungry?

(Happy throws Silk to the gators.)

END OF PLAY

A Little Mystery

WHERE

Morgan and Avery's apartment, where Morgan used to live alone.

WHEN

This afternoon.

CHARACTERS

MORGAN – 20s/30s. Puts others first.

AVERY – 20s/30s. Keeps their cards close to their chest.

These characters can be played by actors of any gender identity.

Morgan and Avery at home.

MORGAN: [. . .] And then my brother accuses me of stealing EVEN THOUGH he's the one who never paid me back like he said he would! And I felt this rage start to burn through my body. Me! Rage! And the phone is shaking in my hand, and finally I'm like it's time to say something.

AVERY: Good for you.

MORGAN: But I lead with an apology and go out of my way to make him feel comfortable and like I'm not attacking him and. Why do I always do that? Why do I always...

(A huge realization)

Oh my God.

AVERY: What?

MORGAN: I always do that. Even when someone's awful to me...and maybe even more so when they are...I put their needs ahead of mine.

(More realization)

Oh God. Like, my boss. Or the one before him. Or the one before her. Wow. Wow. It's like I'm afraid of having people not like me—

AVERY: It's hard when it's work.

MORGAN: No one's forcing me to stay.

AVERY: ...

MORGAN: Wow.

AVERY: ...

MORGAN: Wow.

AVERY: Are you ok?

MORGAN: Yeah, that was just. I feel like an idiot. Wow.

AVERY: …

MORGAN: This is a lot to think about.

AVERY: How do you feel?

MORGAN: Sad. Maybe a little sick.

AVERY: That was really vulnerable.

MORGAN: Sorry.

(Sarcastic)

Aren't you glad you moved in?

AVERY: I'm here 'cause we're kinda serious, you know?

MORGAN: *(Flirting)* Oh, are we?

AVERY: *(Flirting)* Yeah, I don't know if you heard.

MORGAN: I don't have calls like that all the time.

AVERY: I know.

MORGAN: Family.

AVERY: I know.

(Morgan rubs their belly. The "uhhhs" and "mmmms" that follow are them feeling increasing discomfort in their stomach.)

MORGAN: Do you have anything you'd like to, uhhh, you'd like to share?

AVERY: Oh...uh...I didn't realize this was like a show-and-tell kind of thing.

MORGAN: Totally no pressure, but it might, mmm, it might be nice.

AVERY: Sure. I mean. I tend to keep my cards kinda close, you know? It's not you, it's. I mean, when I was still with Kat, she was always saying she felt like she didn't know the real me. Which, I suppose she [didn't]. I mean, I want to. I want to learn how to be open like that, but. It kind of...scares me.

(Breathing heavily, Morgan doubles over slightly. They wipe away a tear or two.

Avery does not notice and feels increasingly guilty for not being equally open.)

Ok, uh. Would it be ok if I took a second to, uh?

(Morgan nods.

Avery, nervous, tries to relax. They take a few deep breaths.)

Ok.

MORGAN: ...

AVERY: Ok.

MORGAN: ...

AVERY: Ok, here goes.

MORGAN: OH GOD. I'M GONNA.

AVERY: It's ok. You can cry.

MORGAN: OH GOD.

AVERY: Sure. Let it out.

MORGAN: I'm really sorry. I don't know how to not make this weird, but I need to go to the bathroom.

AVERY: Oh. Ok.

MORGAN: Sorry. It just hit me.

AVERY: Opening up really opened everything up.

MORGAN: I think it's something I ate.

AVERY: Oh.

MORGAN: Chicken's ok after a couple of weeks, right?

AVERY: No.

MORGAN: But if it's been refrigerated?

AVERY: No.

MORGAN: Suddenly wishing we had moved into your place because there was more space.

AVERY: There's plenty of space here.

MORGAN: I mean so you could go into another room.

AVERY: *(Getting it)* Oh.

MORGAN: ...

AVERY: Should I go get us coffee? Or groceries?

MORGAN: I'll hold it. It's fine.

AVERY: Morgan.

MORGAN: *(In agony)* It's totally fine.

AVERY: This is stupid. We live together now. It's a brave new world. So... So... So...let's be brave.

MORGAN: *(Through tears)* I love you.

AVERY: I love you too. Sweetie, you're crying.

MORGAN: It's because I really need to—

AVERY: Sorry.

MORGAN: I can leave and use the one in the coffee shop or—

AVERY: Go use our bathroom!

(Morgan exits.)

I can be brave too, and uh. Share things about me. If you want. I feel like you've really raised the stakes here with your story. And your, uh...Morgan?

MORGAN: *(Off, clenched)* Yeah, I'm still here.

AVERY: You know what? I'll wait.

MORGAN: *(Clenched)* It's ok. I'm listening.

AVERY: There are things I've never told anyone, because I've been. Well, I was scared. Scared people wouldn't like what they saw when they got to know me, warts and all. Though I don't have warts. Ha! I promise!

MORGAN: *(Clenched)* Thank you for clarifying.

AVERY: I can't do this. This is too weird.

MORGAN: *(Clenched)* If it makes you feel any better...I still haven't gone.

AVERY: ...Oh?

MORGAN: *(Clenched)* I'm too embarrassed.

AVERY: Stop worrying about what other people think!

MORGAN: *(Clenched)* You're not "other people."

AVERY: I know, but—

MORGAN: *(Clenched)* I'm not sure this is how I want to turn over a new leaf.

AVERY: Would it be weird...if we did it at the same time?

MORGAN: *(Clenched)* Yes.

AVERY: ...

MORGAN: *(Clenched)* But I'm game if you are.

AVERY: Uh...

(Avery is suddenly plagued by anxiety about how real this is going to get...and soon! They panic.)

MORGAN: *(Clenched, seeking a yes)* Are you? Are you game, Avery? Avery? Avery? Avery, are you game?

AVERY: I don't, uh.

MORGAN: *(Clenched)* Avery!

AVERY: Alright, on the count of three. One.

MORGAN: *(Clenched)* Here, let me turn the faucet on. Is that better?

AVERY: I don't hear anything.

MORGAN: *(Clenched)* Well, I tried. One.

BOTH: Two.

AVERY: I can't do it! I can't know someone on this level.

MORGAN: ...

AVERY: Morgan?

MORGAN: *(Clenched)* Sorry, can you repeat what you said? I blacked out a little from the—

AVERY: I can't know someone like this! It's too much. I have to go. I'm sorry I'm not brave or adult or. I hope one day you'll forgive me.

MORGAN: *(Clenched)* ...Are you breaking up with me?

AVERY: *(To self)* Oh God.

MORGAN: *(Clenched)* Avery?

AVERY: *(To self)* What's wrong with me?

MORGAN: *(Clenched)* Avery, are you still there?

AVERY: *(To self)* I am a terrible person.

MORGAN: ...Avery?

AVERY: *(To self)* I am shit. I am actual shit.

(Morgan poops. Long, loud, gross.

Now, I'll be honest with you here, dear reader: this moment makes me pretty uncomfortable. It also made most of my writing group uncomfortable when I shared the play for the first time. There's so much shame and anxiety around this thing that we all, as humans, do every day. And for some people, hearing the person they're attracted to make these sounds can be a deal breaker. So, for this moment to work I think it wants it wants to lean into being truly uncomfortable. Less wacky, gross-out comedy and more real. The sorts of sounds that could make Avery feel that they could never look at Morgan the same.

But a sprinkling of a few comedic bells and whistles could be nice. Up to you.

Anyway, back to Morgan pooping.)

MORGAN: I really hope you're gone. I really hope you're not here to—

(Morgan poops more.)

Oh God.

(Eventually, Morgan finishes pooping.

An excruciatingly long pause.

So long.

What a painful pause.

Morgan enters and sees Avery.)

Oh God.

AVERY: Hi.

MORGAN: Oh God. Oh my God.

AVERY: ...

MORGAN: Oh God.

AVERY: At least the windows are open.

MORGAN: I thought you left. Oh God. I'm disgusting. I'm a disgusting person. This is so. Oh God. I should have resisted the chicken, but I. I really needed to eat.

AVERY: ...

MORGAN: Oh God.

AVERY: ...

MORGAN: Oh God.

AVERY: You know, um, for what it's worth: my grandpa never saw my grandma without her makeup on.

MORGAN: ???

AVERY: On my dad's side. Grandpa Joe never saw Grandma Maria when she wasn't done up.

MORGAN: That's insane.

AVERY: They were together for 65 years. She said it was nice knowing there were some things he would never know about her.

MORGAN: Like what her face looked like.

AVERY: Ok, so yeah: it was extreme. But maybe it's just in my blood. A little mystery is nice.

MORGAN: Are you really breaking up with me?

AVERY: No, I mean. No. I'm sorry.

MORGAN: ...

AVERY: ...

MORGAN: You know, you don't have to tell me everything, but it would be nice to be a little more...I would like to know your face.

AVERY: You're looking at it.

MORGAN: You know what I mean.

AVERY: ...

MORGAN: I mean, you've *really* seen my face, so. It can't be worse than that.

(Avery makes a HUGE choice and decides to be vulnerable.)

AVERY: When I was little, I had a lot of confidence. I was smart. I was fearless. My birthday's in August, and the big question was whether I'd be in the same grade as everyone else who was born earlier in the same year as me or whether they'd hold me back. Basically: would I be the youngest or the oldest person in my class? My mom brought me in to meet with Ms. Radnor, the Kindergarten teacher, and she did some tests to see whether it made sense to hold me back. She said it didn't. Developmentally, I was ready to go. Confident little me was raring to get out in the great wide world.

MORGAN: ...

AVERY: But, then I got to school and, I don't know what it was...but maybe the other kids didn't like me or maybe they didn't know *how* to like me...or just didn't *want* to...but...I was marked somehow. The other kids were one team, and I was. I could never be on the inside. And it was a small school. There were, like, 12 of us in my grade. So, I sat at my own end of the cafeteria table. Teachers would make them pick me for teams they didn't want me to be part of. My parents said it would pass. That when people are mean to you it's because someone's been mean to them or they're jealous or scared. But I don't know if that's always true, especially with kids. Sometimes it's just a game. It's fun to have an enemy. It's quite the uniter. Anyway, I got older, and people never really grew out of whatever my parents thought they would. And neither did I. I got to junior high, and it was a bigger school and a chance to start fresh...but I sat alone. Then I started to realize that even the teachers seemed to think something was wrong with me. My grades were fine, but there was this, this general disinterest in me as a person. When I was a junior, I got a job as a cashier at the grocery store, and one day my biology teacher from the year before was at my register and he said hi to me because he recognized me, but he clearly couldn't remember from where. I'd been in his room every day the previous year, but he had to look at my name tag to remember who I was. By then, I'd stopped raising my hand in class, even if I knew an answer. I didn't get involved in any activities. I wanted to. I thought it'd be fun to run track or be in a play. But I was afraid I'd be setting myself up to get hurt. And it always hurt. It always hurt.

MORGAN: ...

AVERY: Now that I'm an adult I guess it's better? Most people ignore everyone around them anyway, so it's easier to just kind of fly under the radar. And people seem to shed their friends as they get older...so maybe I'm lucky because I don't have to feel the loss. The only other person I've really let in was Kat. We were together a few years before she finally made me feel safe enough to let my guard down...which was around the time she fell in love with my roommate. What a coincidence. So, yeah. I'm afraid that if people get to know me, they'll realize that I'm marked. I am a marked person. They'll sense this wrong thing about me that I still don't know what it is. But I know it's there. And, like everyone who came before them, they'll turn away. Anyway, that's something you probably didn't know about me. I was confident once.

(Morgan takes Avery's hand.)

MORGAN: You ok?

AVERY: I feel kind of naked.

MORGAN: How is it?

AVERY: Scary.

MORGAN: That's ok.

AVERY: I'm sorry I made you feel embarrassed.

MORGAN: Forget about it.

AVERY: ...

MORGAN: We'll be ok.

AVERY: Sure.

MORGAN: We will.

AVERY: I hope so.

(Morgan caresses Avery with tender care.)

MORGAN: It's a nice face.

END OF PLAY

Back to School

WHERE

Cold Cross Elementary School. A very, very, very, very, very small school in the very, very, very, very, very small town of Cold Lake, Minnesota.

WHEN

September 1996, morning.

CHARACTERS

BOB – 30s/40s. A substitute gym teacher. One that would have terrified you when you were a kid. Glorious and high status in his youth, now low status and bitter. This is the same Bob from *Man Day*.

THE STUDENTS – PHIL, MARY, APRIL, ZACH, KAREN, WILL

A NOTE ON THE TEXT

It's more important that we're focused on Bob's journey than on the silliness of adults playing kids. The student lines will get laughs—I promise—but it's crucial that Bob's longing melancholy isn't drowned out. Perhaps the students are only offstage voices or played by a single actor.

This play is set in rural Minnesota, and as such it's helpful if the characters speak with thick working-class MN accents reminiscent of *Fargo* or *Drop Dead Gorgeous*.

PREMIERE

Back to School was originally performed as part of *From Cold Lake: Episode 2*, which received its world premiere at The Peoples Improv Theater (Ali Reza Farahnakian, Founder and Caretaker; Stephen Stout, Artistic Director) in New York City on September 12th, 2016. The producers were Matt Cox, Kristin McCarthy Parker and Stephen Stout. It was directed by Colin Waitt. Songs and Score were composed by Tommy Crawford. Sound design & mixing was by Matt Cox. The cast was as follows:

BOB: Patrick McCartney
STUDENTS: Nick Abeel, Maggie Delgadillo, Kullan Edberg, Alex Haynes

A bell rings.

Bob claps the students to their seats like your worst nightmare of a coach.

BOB: Alright, take your seats. Take your seats.

(He blows aggressively into his whistle.)

I SAID SIT DOWN. Welcome to the sixth grade. Mrs. Kunkel just had a baby, so they've promoted me from substitute gym teacher to substitute your teacher until she's back. Hopefully she'll return right around the time you all have to learn where babies like hers come from, 'cause who has two thumbs and did not sign up for that crap?

(Pause. Bob is shocked no one answered)

The answer is this guy.

(Silence.)

This guy is me.

(Silence.)

Do we have Phil Albrecht?
PHIL: Here.
BOB: Mary Benson.
MARY: Here.
BOB: April Benson.
APRIL: Present.
BOB: Present. Jesus. Um, Zach Lange.
ZACH: I'm here Coach Schmidtbauer.
BOB: There he is.

(They do a very cool, very specific handshake.)

Zach just led the Cold Lake Leeches to victory in the little league tournament. And what did the rest of you do with your summers?
APRIL: I created a special filtration system that will hopefully make it easier for people in developing countries to have access to clean water.

BOB: That's enough out of you, April Benson. How ya doin', Zach?

ZACH: Ya know. Whatever.

BOB: Who's next? Karen Schultz?

KAREN: *(Lisp, probably too excited)* Here! You like my new braces?!

BOB: You have something leafy for breakfast today, Karen?

KAREN: My mom made me my favorite: spinach!

BOB: Will Weber—

KAREN: I grew it myself!

BOB: Ok, Karen.

KAREN: Spinach for breakfast! What a treat!

BOB: Karen, just [shut up]. Will Weber.

WILL: Here.

BOB: And yup. That's the whole grade. Great. Anyway, happy first day of school. The town council told the administration to tell me I have to read you this inspirational statement, so ok. Here we go.

(He reads.)

"Imagine a version of yourself sitting in a chair kinda like the one you're in now...only it's two hundred years ago and you're probably dressed like Laura Ingalls Wilder and her family. Just picture it: the mud, the blizzards, the dysentery. Are you picturing it? Good. Now imagine the Laura Ingalls Wilder version of yourself imagining you here today. What would they find surprising? We bet they never imagined that instead of going blind from disease that bowl cuts would become a thing. Pause for laughter.

(Pause.)

We think you'll agree that a lot can happen in two hundred years. And a lot can happen in a single year too. As you embark on your final year of studies here at Cold Cross Elementary School, we encourage you to make today even more wonderful than the dysentery-riddled Laura Ingalls Wilder version of you could have imagined...and an even better memory for the version of you sitting there two hundred years in the future, who may actually be a robot, or at least a cryogenically frozen head.

(To himself)

That was a complicated sentence to say.

(*Reading*)

"Make it a great first day of school. Life is yours for the taking."

(He crumples up the paper.)

Pfff. Who the heck wrote that and what planet were they from? What they really should have said was:

(A little too intensely)

"Welcome to the sixth grade, aka your last year at Cold Cross Elementary School. Your grandparents probably never made it this far because they had to work on their farms, your parents were here like you and look where it got them, and next year you'll be shipped off to St. Cloud where now you'll have a class size of at least 1000, so no pressure, but good luck."

(Bob crumples the paper and throws it toward the garbage can but misses.)

KAREN: Mr. Schmidtbauer, you missed the garbage.
BOB: And you look like a mulcher exploded in your mouth, Karen Schultz, so why don't you shut it.

(He puts the paper in the garbage as he talks to himself.)

And I've lost the will to [live]—
WILL: I'm here, Mr. Schmidtbauer.
BOB: What?
WILL: You said you lost the will, but I'm Will. And I'm here.
BOB: ...
WILL: Please don't mark me absent.
ZACH: Coach Schmidtbauer, is it true you went to Cold Cross Elementary School?
BOB: It is, Zach. This is where I met my wife.
APRIL: What did you want to be when you were our age?
BOB: What's that, April?

APRIL: When you were a kid, what did you want to be?

BOB: You mean you don't think this is what I wanted? Don't answer that.

(Small pause.)

Oh, I don't know.

(Small pause.)

I wanted to go to space.

APRIL: Have you done it?

BOB: Gone to space?

APRIL: Yeah.

BOB: It's a good thing you're interested in water filters and not brain surgery, April Benson. You can't just go into space.

APRIL: You could be an astronaut.

BOB: Yah. Well.

APRIL: Why didn't you become one of them?

BOB: Because, April, contrary to popular belief, you can't just do whatever you want in life.

APRIL: Sure you can.

BOB: You can't.

APRIL: You can. You just go.

BOB: *(Sarcastic)* Gosh, April, you're right. I should have just gone. Forget the grades or getting into a fancy school or having money. None of that should have stopped me. All I needed was a strong enough will.

WILL: I'm still here, Mr. Schmidtbauer.

BOB: I know, Will.

WILL: Please don't mark me absent.

BOB: If there's one thing I hope you all learn from me, it's that life will let you down. And that is disappointing. Oh man is that disappointing. I know everyone likes to think they're unique, but as someone who sat in those chairs where you are and knows where everyone around him ended up, take it from me: don't dream too big. You'll only hurt yourself.

(A pause.)

Now, who wants to watch a movie?

THE CLASS: Me!

KAREN: What's the movie?

BOB: It's the Academy Award winning masterpiece *Forest Gump*.

(Groans and disgust from the class.)

What would you rather watch?

(They all shout out movies from the early to mid 90s. Little Mermaid, Aladdin, Beauty & the Beast, Home Alone, Beethoven. One of them calls out The Silence of the Lambs. It gets overwhelming.)

Ok, enough! Enough!

(He puts the tape in the VCR.)

It's already in so I guess we'll have to watch it.

(The movie begins to play.)

At the start, there's a feather that flies around for a while and you'll probably think, "This is stupid," which admittedly it kinda is. But then you'll watch the story of a man who lives through most of the major events of the twentieth century and think, "Now that's a life."

(Sadly)

That is. A life.

(He grabs the hall pass, which is probably made of wood.)

I'll be back in a few minutes. You can't come looking, because I have the hall pass.

(He beings to leave.

Then, enraptured by the opening credits, he stops to watch.

He stands a few moments, moved and transfixed.

He wipes a tear away.

Then, suddenly aware of the students, he leaves.)

END OF PLAY

Let's Get Weird

WHERE

Trish's home in the very, very, very, very, very small town of Cold Lake, Minnesota. Likely an abundance of animal knick-knacks and sayings painted on wood ("Bless This Mess").

WHEN

Tonight.

CHARACTERS

TRISH – 30s/40s. Nice, but not the brightest crayon in the box.
PATTY – 30s/40s. Knows she's better than this stupid, stupid town.

A NOTE ON THE TEXT

Though the rest of the plays set in Cold Lake in this collection take place in the mid-nineties, I imagine this one to take place today. Trish's nephew, Hunter, is the same character featured in *Man Day*.

INSPIRATION

This play was inspired by the world of my radio play, *From Cold Lake*. As you've probably clocked by now, it was the basis for a few works in this anthology. Though this is a new piece, the wonderful actors that originated these characters were very much in my mind as I wrote it. So, I wanted to credit them here.

TRISH: Maggie Delgadillo
PATTY: Kullan Edberg

A knock at the door.

Trish answers. Patty stands, vaping. She holds a case of booze.

TRISH: Patty! You came!

(Trish hugs Patty too tightly.)

Yay! Girls' night!

(Still hugging Patty, Trish begins to jump up and down in celebration.)

This is going to be so much fun!!!!

PATTY: Suck a skunk, Trish. It's not that I'm butt hurt the rest of the she-devils of Cold Lake didn't invite me to the cookie exchange.

TRISH: *(Still jumping for joy)* I'm not gonna say I'm not hurt.

PATTY: I mean, who cares how many variations of those sugar cookies with the giant chocolate drop Sue or Lorraine can do?

TRISH: We don't normally vape in the [house].

PATTY: I'm just offended the only other person they didn't invite was you.

TRISH: Yeah, what's that about? You think they have something against people named Patricia?

PATTY: Probably. Lotta small minds around here.

TRISH: Maybe they're just jealous you're cool and cultured.

PATTY: I am very cool and cultured.

TRISH: You are. You drink wine, you follow the Academy Awards.

PATTY: It's true.

TRISH: Am I cool and cultured too?

PATTY: That's a no, Trish.

TRISH: But I wasn't invited either...so maybe a little?

PATTY: Bartender, I'll have a Cosmopolitan.

TRISH: Ok! How do I make that?

PATTY: It's vodka, triple sec, cranberry and lime juice. Duh.

(Trish assembles what she needs.)

TRISH: On it!

PATTY: But for mine, I don't need the cranberry or lime or triple sec. And substitute tequila for vodka.

TRISH: *(Confused)* Ok, so I'll...?

PATTY: Just pour some tequila in a glass, Trish.

TRISH: I'll have the same!

(Trish pours tequila into two glasses. They toast.)

Yay Cosmopolitans!

(They shoot them. Trish is overwhelmed by the tequila's burn.)

Fancy.

PATTY: Bartender, another.

(Trish preps a second round. Patty vapes.)

TRISH: You know, Patty, maybe we can stop vaping for a while?

PATTY: You're killing me here.

TRISH: No, you're killing you here. With your vape.

(Patty does the biggest eye roll as she puts her vape pen away.

They do another shot. Trish squirms uncomfortably from the taste.)

I can't believe they drink these in *Sex and the City*.

PATTY: *(Wistful)* Oh, New York...

TRISH: Patty...have you ever wanted to—?

PATTY: I don't want to go to New York with you, Trish.

TRISH: That's fine, because I don't want to go to New York never ever never. No, what I was going to ask was…have you ever wanted to do something…not nice?

PATTY: Should we slash Sue and Lorraine's tires?

TRISH: No, but. No. No. But. I have this book.

PATTY: Stop trying to sell me on your book club, Trish.

TRISH: I'm not. Though, if you ever change your mind, you're welcome to join me any Tuesday at The Cold Lake Ladies Home Book Club.

PATTY: I'd rather chew glass.

TRISH: Now don't worry—we aren't feminist.

(Patty downs another drink.)

The Cold Lake Ladies Home Book Club welcomes all women, except feminists. It's not that we don't like them, we just generally don't agree with their ideas or insanity. Girl power! Are you ok?

PATTY: *(Dying inside, getting her back on subject)* Trish, you have a book?

TRISH: I do! It's a. Well, it's a book of. It's magic. It's a magic book.

PATTY: Like, magic tricks?

TRISH: Like magic spells. My nephew, Hunter—you know Hunter, right?

PATTY: Yeah.

TRISH: With the piercings and the rings and the robes? He's, he's, he's, what's the word?

PATTY: Gay?

TRISH: I was going to say, "a witch."

PATTY: He's a gay witch?

TRISH: He doesn't have time for a girlfriend. He's too busy casting spells. Anyway, I'm not normally into that sort of thing, but, well, he left it here and I was sitting there thinking about not being invited to the cookie exchange, and it just kind of fell open in my hand. And then my hand just kind of happened to turn the pages and next thing I know I'm holding a, well, it's a spell for vengeance. Now, you know me. I'm not a vengeful person. I just need a wine cooler and a book that's not feminist and I'm set. But I do think it's kind of—what's the word? It's not <u>nice</u> that literally all of the other women in town are together exchanging cookies and it's just me and you, a very cultured though not always nice, um. What am I trying to say?

PATTY: Get to the point, Trish.

TRISH: I can see why they might not like you. But me? <u>Me</u>? That's just. <u>Me</u>?! So, yeah. I don't think it's nice and it makes me feel not nice things and I was thinking maybe we could try to...do you want to cast a spell of vengeance?

PATTY: Watch out, world. Trish Schaeffer is fired up.

TRISH: I'm very composed.

PATTY: It's ok, Trish. Be mad!

TRISH: I'm not mad. Emotions should be buried like septic tanks. ...So, what do you say?

PATTY: I thought tonight was gonna suck, so YEAH! Let's get weird.

(Trish opens the book and reads the spell, doing everything as she says it.)

TRISH: Ok, I'm opening the book, and it says sprinkle a little salt, and keep your cinnamon broom nearby—look, I made this one special for the occasion. Tassels courtesy of Crafts Direct. Then it says "sit."

PATTY: You don't need to narrate.

TRISH: So, do you want to read the incantation or should I?

PATTY: You're the one holding the cinnamon broom, Trish. I think you should do the honors.

TRISH: You know, people may say bad things about you behind your back, Patty. And they do. But the one thing they can't say is that you don't have good manners. Anyway.

(Reading)

"Dear Lord Satan."

PATTY: Uh, what?

TRISH: "Dear Lord Satan, burst forth from us like a beast out of hell." Little more intense than I was expecting. "We are your demon spawn. Fill us with your musky breath and speak through us so that vengeance may be served in your name." Well, no *Chicken Soup for the Pet Lover's Soul*, but it's something. Patty? ...Patty?

(Patty stares off, as in a trance.

When she speaks, the quality of her voice has changed.)

PATTY: **Patty is no longer here, thou fool.**

TRISH: Oh my gosh.

PATTY: **It is I, Lord Satan.**

TRISH: It worked!

PATTY: **Silence, fool. Dost thou wish for vengeance?**

TRISH: Can I have a minute to think about it?

PATTY: **Thou summonest me. Isn't this what thou wants?**

TRISH: Yes, but it's a little more intense than I was expecting.

PATTY: **Thou will have vengeance or thine soul is mine.**

TRISH: Ok, vengeance sounds great.

PATTY: **Vengeance shalt rain down on Lorraine and Sue and it wilt be very not nice.**

TRISH: Goodie!

PATTY: **And all it will cost...is your soul.**

TRISH: *(Clarifying)* Wait, I thought you said I had to do this or you'd take my [soul]?

PATTY: **Ok, fine. Thou drivest a hard bargain, Fool. Thou mayest keep thine soul if and only if...you let Patty Bauer vape in your home.**

TRISH: Fine! Deal! Patty can vape as much as she likes.

PATTY: *(As self)* Thanks, Trish. Real generous of you.

(Trish immediately understands she's been lied to.

Patty vapes profusely.)

TRISH: Oh, I see. Patty, put out your vape.

PATTY: It's not a cigarette, Trish.

TRISH: Then unplug it or turn it off or—

PATTY: I can't help it if I'm cool and cultured and Lord Satan said I should be allowed to vape in thine home.

TRISH: This is. This is why you weren't invited to exchange cookies.

PATTY: Because of Satan?

TRISH: Because you're a mean person. You're mean and a snob and who can blame anyone for not liking you?

(This stings Patty.)

PATTY: Well, you weren't invited either, Trish.

TRISH: I know, and I got a lot going on for me. I have a green thumb, I don't care for New York and I read books that aren't feminist. But I guess they associate me with you, which is. I thought it was cool when we were kids, but now I. I think you should leave.

(Trish holds open the door.)

PATTY: Trish, lighten up.

TRISH: ...

PATTY: Have another Cosmopolitan and let's...

(Patty pours them each a tequila shot.)

Let's party like it's the Independent Spirit Awards.

(She hands Trish a shot and toasts. Patty downs her shot. Trish does not drink hers.

Patty lightly pries Trish off the door and shuts it, vaping. Trish continues to be annoyed about the vape.)

Let's just. Let's try a different spell. Here, this one is called Spell for Vengeance II. Here, you just sit back. Sip your cosmo, and—

TRISH: Can I have a real one?

PATTY: Sit back, / and.

TRISH: I want a real / cosmo.

PATTY: I'll read it, and everything will be. Ok, here goes. "Dear Lord Satan." Really leaning into a theme here. "Dear Lord Satan. Ruin the lives of those who've done us wrong."

TRISH: Ruin them.

PATTY: "Make them suffer."

TRISH: Yes.

PATTY: Not sure we need the call and response, Trish. "Make their agony consume them until they are nothing. And may it hurt."

TRISH: Hurt them.

PATTY: "In your name we scream."

(Patty doesn't scream but makes an unforced sound that hints toward one. Trish, on the other hand, lets out a very intense, almost primal roar of a scream. She really means it. She lets out all of her repressed rage at Patty, Lorraine, Sue, everyone.)

Ok, Trish. That's [a bit much].

(Trish is still screaming.

She finishes.

They wait a beat.)

Ok, Trish, I'm gonna [go home].

(Suddenly, Trish collapses as though propelled by an unseen force.

Patty runs to her.)

Trish!

(Trish rises fiercely and throws Patty off of her.

Her voice is changed. She is a woman possessed.)

TRISH: **Get your grubby hands off me.**

PATTY: Ow, Trish. That hurt.

TRISH: **You rang?**

PATTY: Trish, let go of my arm.

TRISH: **Trish has left the building.**

PATTY: Trish, this is stupid.

TRISH: **I said the simp is no longer here.**

> *(Trish reaches out and an unseen force radiates from her hands. It pins Patty to the wall.)*

PATTY: *(Realizing this is real)* Holy shit.

TRISH: **Bitch, please. Ain't nothing holy about me. Now, what do you want?**

PATTY: I don't, uh.

TRISH: **You better not have called me without a reason. 'Cause that would be a stupid thing to do.**

PATTY: Wow.

TRISH: **What?!**

PATTY: I just can't believe you're actually [real]. Wow. Wow.

TRISH: **Get to the point before I rip out your spine.**

PATTY: Will you really rain down vengeance?

TRISH: **Say the name.**

PATTY: ...

TRISH: **Don't waste my time.**

PATTY: Destroy them. Everyone in Cold Lake.

TRISH: **All of them?**

PATTY: Wipe 'em off the face of the earth.

TRISH: **What you thinking? Electrical fire? Nuclear meltdown?**

PATTY: Dealer's choice.

(Trish smiles and snaps her fingers.)

TRISH: **Done.**

(A deep rumbling. Patty is almost knocked over.)

PATTY: What was that?

TRISH: **You'll see. Now my payment.**

PATTY: Wait! I—

TRISH: **I'm not an intern. I don't work for free.**

PATTY: Hold on. I didn't realize this would happen so [quickly]—

TRISH: **You will spend eternity with me, which I think at this point goes without saying.**

PATTY: Hold on.

TRISH: **But first: the rest of your life.**

PATTY: Please. Can I take it back?

TRISH: **Silence.**

(Patty cowers, terrified.)

You will remain trapped in what's left of this stupid small town. You'll spend the rest of your life surrounded by idiots who have no interest in anything you enjoy. In fact, not only will they dislike everything that makes you happy...they'll judge you for it. And then one day—just for fun—you will finally make it to the big city...but the joke will be on you...for the people there will see you as the uncultured hick you are. You are nothing, Patty Bauer. You have always been nothing. And you will remain nothing until the day you are mine.

PATTY: Please.

TRISH: **But you can keep Trish.**
PATTY: Please, don't hurt any—
TRISH: **Thank you for your purchase.**

(Satan exits Trish's body, which leaves her crumpled on the floor.)

PATTY: I take it back! I take it back!

(Trish begins to stir.)

TRISH: Ow...the Cosmos really went to my head.
PATTY: ...
TRISH: It's a shame the spells didn't work. I guess what did I expect from
    my nephew, the witch? He does have nice robes, though.
PATTY: ...
TRISH: Is something burning?

(Trish goes to the window.)

Holy crap the town is on fire! Holy crap!
PATTY: I'm sorry, Trish.
TRISH: Holy crap! We gotta call 911!

(Trish dials her phone.)

PATTY: I'm sorry for vaping. I'm sorry for—
TRISH: Patty, now is not the—Hello? I need to report an emergency.

(Patty pages though the book.)

PATTY: How do I take it back?

(Trish rips the book out of Patty's hands.)

TRISH: Patty, enough.

(Into phone, exiting)

There's fire everywhere. No, I don't know how it—Oh my gosh, I
hope my family's alright!

(Trish is gone. Trembling, Patty pulls out her vape pen.)

PATTY: Please. I take it back. I take it all back.

(Suddenly repulsed by the idea of the vape pen, Patty tosses it away from herself.)

END OF PLAY

Pilot Light

WHERE

The front yard of Danielle and Savannah's childhood home in rural Minnesota.

WHEN

A January morning.

CHARACTERS

DANIELLE – 20s/30s. The older sister. The golden child. Has left the area and has a nice job.

SAVANNAH – 20s/30s. The younger sister. The rebellious one. Likely with dyed hair, tattoos, piercings. Has never left their hometown.

A NOTE ON THE TEXT

Though this play is set in rural Minnesota, I think that overdoing the accents will likely detract from the weight of the story. If you decide to do them, keep them light.

"Niedemeyer," as in Mary Niedemeyer, is pronounced "Knee-deh-meyer."

PREMIERE

A version of *Pilot Light* that was both exactly the same and completely different to the one presented here received its world premiere as part of *Rule of 7 x 7* (Brett Epstein, Producer) at The Tank (Rosalind Grush and Rania Jumaily, Co-Artistic Directors) in New York City on April 24th, 2015. It was directed by David Monteagudo. Tech was by Elizabeth Strauss.

The actors were Evan Maltby, Zac Moon and Ryan Stinnett

The play that follows owes a great deal to that original production and its team.

Savannah and Danielle stand looking at their childhood home, which is somewhere behind the audience.

Danielle occasionally rubs her hands for warmth.

They notice someone driving past.

DANIELLE: What is Mary Niedemeyer up to now?

SAVANNAH: She got a snowplow.

DANIELLE: I see that.

SAVANNAH: Mom said Mary appointed herself the official plower of County Road 8. Said an alien told her it was her destiny.

DANIELLE: That is a person who votes.

SAVANNAH: Mary Niedemeyer is so weird.

DANIELLE: So weird. You think she's gonna tell mom's guardian she saw us?

SAVANNAH: Donna won't care we're here.

DANIELLE: Pretty sure mom's guardian might care when the house burns down.

SAVANNAH: Dude, you can call Donna by her name.

DANIELLE: Should have come at night.

SAVANNAH: I wouldn't have got the court to appoint her if she was a monster.

DANIELLE: Feels like a bad sign we've already been seen.

(They wave stoically at Mary as she vanishes down the road.)

SAVANNAH: ...

DANIELLE: ...

SAVANNAH: ...

DANIELLE: So, who's gonna do it?

SAVANNAH: ...

DANIELLE: ...

SAVANNAH: We could flip a coin.

DANIELLE: I don't carry cash.

SAVANNAH: I have one.

DANIELLE: Why?

SAVANNAH: What do you mean, "why?" I use money.

DANIELLE: Forget it.

SAVANNAH: You want heads or tails?

DANIELLE: Forget I brought it up.

SAVANNAH: I brought it up.

DANIELLE: Just put the coin away.

SAVANNAH: Heads I do it, tails you—

DANIELLE: It won't work.

SAVANNAH: It's the perfect way to randomly pick between two—

DANIELLE: Stop with the coin. Enough with the coin.

SAVANNAH: Dude, why are you—

DANIELLE: I don't want to. I don't want to do it. I don't want to burn the house down. I don't want to be the one to do it. I'm not gonna do it.

SAVANNAH: Well, one of us has gotta—

DANIELLE: Put the coin away.

(Fuming, Savannah puts the coin away.)

Anyway, you hunt. You should do it.

SAVANNAH: What?

DANIELLE: You like to kill things.

SAVANNAH: Shooting a deer is not the same as burning down mom's house.

DANIELLE: It's adjacent.

SAVANNAH: Are you trying to force me to do it?

DANIELLE: No.

SAVANNAH: You totally are.

DANIELLE: I mean, if you want to.

SAVANNAH: Why don't you? It was your idea.

DANIELLE: Exactly. I already made my contribution.

SAVANNAH: You're an idiot.

DANIELLE: You are.

SAVANNAH: You are.

DANIELLE: You are.

SAVANNAH: You are.

(Danielle whacks Savannah upside the head.

Savannah whacks her back.

They keep hitting each other: two petulant sisters.)

DANIELLE: You suck!

SAVANNAH: "You suck?!" What are you, twelve?!

DANIELLE: You're the one who called me an idiot!

SAVANNAH: Because you are!

DANIELLE: You suck!

SAVANNAH: You suck!

DANIELLE: *(Backing away)* Alright alright alright enough. This is stupid. I never should have come back.

SAVANNAH: That's a mouthful.

DANIELLE: Shut up.

SAVANNAH: You shut up, city girl.

DANIELLE: City girl? What is this, a movie from the fifties?

SAVANNAH: Yeah, a real obscure one that only you've seen.

DANIELLE: SHUT. UP.

SAVANNAH: Tell us about it so we know you're better than us.

DANIELLE: *(Under her breath)* This is why mom stopped talking to you.

SAVANNAH: What did you say?

DANIELLE: ...

SAVANNAH: *(Murderous)* What did you say?

DANIELLE: Nothing.

SAVANNAH: ...

DANIELLE: ...

SAVANNAH: ...

DANIELLE: ...

SAVANNAH: She's not talking to you either.

DANIELLE: I know.

SAVANNAH: So don't make this about.

DANIELLE: I know. Sorry.

SAVANNAH: ...

DANIELLE: I'm sorry.

SAVANNAH: ...

DANIELLE: ...

SAVANNAH: All you gotta do is go up to the furnace—

DANIELLE: Or you. It could be you.

SAVANNAH: All one of us hasta do is go to the furnace, find the pilot light, and blow.

DANIELLE: ...

SAVANNAH: *(To both of them)* Just go...

(Neither of them moves. They continue to stare at the house.)

DANIELLE: Typical Olsons.

(A long silence.

Mary Niedemeyer drives past again.)

DANIELLE: She is really going for it.

SAVANNAH: There's not even snow left to plow.

DANIELLE: Mary Neidemeyer is so weird.

SAVANNAH: So weird.

(They watch Mary go, turning as she passes.

Just as she's about to leave, they give her a little wave.)

DANIELLE: To have been a fly on the wall when Mary found mom.

SAVANNAH: God, can you imagine?

DANIELLE: It was the mail in the mailbox, right?

SAVANNAH: Yeah, it was overflowing.

DANIELLE: Just picture mom being like, "What in the hell is crazy Mary Neidemeyer doing here with all that mail?"

SAVANNAH: And Mary wondering if the naked lady laying in feces is dead. Turns out mom drinks mouth wash now.

DANIELLE: What?

SAVANNAH: When the vodka runs out. She may not have made it to the toilet, but she made it to the cabinet under the sink. So, she was satiated.

(Beat.)

Mary's dad was an alcoholic too, so I guess she'd been, uh. I guess she'd been keeping an eye out.

DANIELLE: Whatever happened to the tree house?

SAVANNAH: *(Pointing)* It's still there.

DANIELLE: It's held together pretty well.

SAVANNAH: Mmm.

DANIELLE: You were always good with stuff like that.

SAVANNAH: Thanks.

DANIELLE: Was it always so small?

SAVANNAH: Mmm.

DANIELLE: I don't remember it being so small.

SAVANNAH: ...

DANIELLE: Who'd have ever thought?

SAVANNAH: ...

DANIELLE: There's no escape, is there?

SAVANNAH: Donna has to sell everything to pay for the medical bills and the treatment facility.

DANIELLE: I still can't believe mom has a guardian.

SAVANNAH: Then after treatment it's the what-do-they-call it? The step-down facility. Then assisted living, or. I dunno. Wherever mom ends up.

DANIELLE: You've really stayed in the loop.

SAVANNAH: You're welcome to participate whenever.

DANIELLE: Would have been nice to inherit something.

SAVANNAH: I'm sure you'll be fine.

DANIELLE: Would have been nice for you.

SAVANNAH: Well, at least we get to lose everything on our own terms.

DANIELLE: What a win.

SAVANNAH: Oh mom.

DANIELLE: ...

SAVANNAH: ...

DANIELLE: ...

SAVANNAH: ...

(Danielle pulls out a coin. Savannah is a bit surprised.)

DANIELLE: Heads you do it, tails it's me.

(Danielle tosses the coin and catches it.

She flips it to her arm.

She lifts her hand.

They look at the result.

The gravity of the moment washes over them.

Danielle rubs her hands nervously.

Then, she goes inside the house.

Savannah watches her go, suddenly feeling very exposed.

Mary Niedemeyer drives past.

Savannah tries to avoid her gaze.

Unseen, Mary waves at her.

Savannah avoids Mary's gaze...but Mary keeps waving...so Savannah finally has to give her an awkward, small wave.

An eternity seems to pass.

Finally, Danielle reenters.

They stare at the house.)

DANIELLE: I guess that's it.
SAVANNAH: ...
DANIELLE: ...
SAVANNAH: ...
DANIELLE: Should we run or something?
SAVANNAH: It'll be a while 'til there's enough gas to be dangerous.
DANIELLE: ...
SAVANNAH: ...
DANIELLE: ...

SAVANNAH: ...

DANIELLE: A classic Minnesota goodbye. Everyone wants to leave.
Nobody makes a move.

(They stand in silence, watching the house fill with gas.)

DANIELLE: Goodbye, house.
SAVANNAH: Goodbye.

END OF PLAY

Hot Dog Eat Dog

I originally wrote this play because I wanted something I could submit to competitions that felt like "Peak Colin Waitt." So, here you have it: small lives, huge stakes, rural Minnesota, bizarro personal histories and a lot of sadness underneath the funny. In the context of this anthology, I suppose nothing much has changed. The play never won or was a finalist for anything, so I guess "Peak Colin Waitt" isn't for everyone. But it inspired me to create a full-length play, *Fair*, which includes *Tunnel of Love* and *The Miracle of Birth*. Lemons; lemonade. I'm not sure how you'd actually stage *Hot Dog Eat Dog*, as I think it truly wants to feel like the contestants are eating an obscene number of hot dogs. But I hope some brave souls will give it a try because Karen Larsen-Overbauer-Klein and the rest of these weirdos are some of my favorite creations.

WHERE

A hot dog eating contest at a county fair in rural Minnesota. A long table set up with plastic cups, hot dogs, and signs that count how many hot dogs each contestant has eaten. Lots of red, white and blue. The patriotism is overwhelming. To the side, an announcer's booth that broadcasts live on local public access television. Low-fi and perhaps a touch dated.

WHEN

Today.

CHARACTERS

KAREN LARSEN-OVERBAUER-KLEIN
CHUCK
MARY LOU
AMBER
MITCH
LORRAINE
JUDGE

A NOTE ON THE TEXT

This play is set in rural Minnesota, and as such it's helpful if the characters speak with thick working-class MN accents reminiscent of *Fargo* or *Drop Dead Gorgeous*.

"Klaver," as in Local Artist Linda Klaver, rhymes with "Waiver."

Low rent public broadcasting intro music plays. Retro. Cheerful.

Two local broadcasters sit at their desk. They are Karen Larsen-Overbauer-Klein and Chuck.

Behind them, a table set up for a hot dog eating contest.

KAREN: Greetings from between the knitting booth and the tunnel of love! We are coming to you live from the Benton County Qualifier for the Minnesota State Hot Dog Eating Contest, presented by Larsen-Overbauer-Klein Flooring! I'm Karen Larsen-Overbauer-Klein of Larsen-Overbauer-Klein Flooring.

CHUCK: And I'm Chuck. Like Beyoncé or Sting, but Chuck.

KAREN: It is a beautiful day, and we thank you for spending it indoors watching us on your TV.

(Karen gestures, showing off a giant ring. She clearly wants Chuck to notice it, though she feigns nonchalance.)

CHUCK: What a shiny ring.

KAREN: Thank you. It's from Missouri.

CHUCK Today's champion will go on to represent Benton County in the State tournament later this summer.

KAREN: *(Re: ring)* Is it too much?

CHUCK: Karen, why don't you, uh, why don't you tell us a little bit about our sponsor?

KAREN: I thought you'd never ask. "From granite to ceramic to wood to carpet...whatever your flooring needs, Larsen-Overbauer-Klein Flooring will FLOOR you with our expertise." I know. [The pun] It's good. And FOR THIS MONTH ONLY, ALL FLOORS at Larsen-Overbauer-Klein Flooring are BUY ONE, GET ONE.

CHUCK: Buy one get one free? That's pretty great.

KAREN: No. You buy one and you get the one you bought.

CHUCK: I've just received word they're starting the weigh-in, so let's go to Mary Lou Olmstead, who is down there with our competitors.

(Mary Lou appears.)

Mary Lou?

MARY LOU: Hi!

CHUCK: How're things down there?

MARY LOU: Great! I'm here with reigning local champion, Amber "The Iron Jaw" Hutchinson.

(Amber is basically a gladiator.)

AMBER: Hey.

MARY LOU: Two years ago, Amber set the local record for number of hot dogs eaten: 39. Now, most competitors dip theirs in water for ease of swallow, but not "The Iron Jaw."

AMBER: I do it dry.

MARY LOU: She is also the reigning Lumberjack Games Champion, Captain of the Sartell Women's Softball Team and can lift a tractor tire over her head. Amber, how do you feel going into today?

(Amber lets out an intense, long gladiatorial battle cry. If this were a cartoon, the sound would probably knock Mary Lou over. But this is not a cartoon...so she just takes it.

A tiny pause.)

(WTF) Ok. Best of luck today, Amber.

(Amber lets out another battle cry as she exits to get weighed.

Mitch enters. He is basically a mean old man.)

Next up, we have Mitch Kunkel. Hi, Mitch!

MITCH: No need to yell, I'm right here.

MARY LOU: This is a bit of a homecoming for you today, isn't it?

MITCH: I've come to reclaim what's...Ruth?

(Mitch stares into space, lost in memory)

MARY LOU: Mr. Kunkel? Mr. Kunkel? Uh...

(Mary Lou waves her hands in front of his unresponsive face.)

KAREN: *(Aside)* It's been a rough year for Mitch Kunkel. I don't want to gossip, but his wife left him for a younger man. She's one of them, what do ya call 'ems?

CHUCK: Cougars?

KAREN: Yeah, but what do you call it when she's a cougar, but the younger man actually looks older?

CHUCK: Like Benjamin Button?

KAREN: Kinda. Except he's not Brad Pitt, he's just a really actually not very attractive eighteen-year-old who looks and smells like he's about eighty. What's that called?

CHUCK: ...I don't think there's a word for that.

KAREN: Well, that's what happened. Not to gossip.

(Mary Lou gives Mitch a poke.

And another.)

(Still aside) And then Mitch lost his job. And his retirement. And his home. Not to gossip.

MARY LOU: *(Moving on)* Ok, well maybe I should—

(Mitch snaps out of whatever spell he was under.)

MITCH: RUTHIE, DON'T LEAVE ME. I'LL DO ANYTHING. Oh. You're not Ruth.

MARY LOU: You alright, Mr. Kunkel?

MITCH: 'Course I am. Why would you ask?

MARY LOU: You kinda went away for a second there.

MITCH: Well, you're a deluded person. What was I saying?

MARY LOU: You were saying you've come to reclaim / what's.

MITCH: I've come to reclaim what's mine. I was the local hot dog champion all of my adult life. Nobody could touch "The Meat Grinder." And then two years ago a certain tractor tire lifting phony waltzed in here, ate 39 wieners and took what belonged to me. I'll be damned if I let it happen again. "The Meat Grinder" is back, baby!

(Mitch exits, pumping his fists.)

MARY LOU: Ooo. Stakes.

CHUCK: They're actually hot dogs, not steaks, Mary Lou.

MARY LOU: And last but not least, we have Lorraine Baasch.

(Lorraine enters. She has a real Allison Janney energy about her.)

LORRAINE: That's Baasch with two a-s. In case you put it, ya know, put it on your screen. So they can [read it]. All my life. Name misspelled. What a pain it makes me feel right here in my [heart] whatdoyacallit.

MARY LOU: Heart?

LORRAINE: That is the thing in my chest, yes.

MARY LOU: Lorraine Baasch with two a-s, what got you interested in eating hot dogs in the first place?

LORRAINE: When I gave up smoking, I filled that void with eating hot dogs. Went from two packs a day to two packs a day, if you know what I mean.

MARY LOU: 'Cause they're / hot dogs.

LORRAINE: 'Cause they're hot dogs, yah. Then I worked my way up to three then four then five. It's a lot of hot dogs, but hey: sure beats lung cancer.

(She coughs some very wet coughs then leaves.)

MARY LOU: And just a friendly reminder to everyone out there lining up to join us today to make sure you're in the correct line. We're right next door to the Miracle of Birth Barn, and the entrances look remarkably similar. Adding to the confusion, Latoya Gunderson's dog is currently giving birth to puppies. Hot dogs, baby dogs. But just not the same, ya know?

KAREN: Do we know what kind of puppies they'll be?

MARY LOU: Latoya's dog is a Pomeranian, and I guess she bred it with a Pit Bull.

KAREN: Pom Bulls. My favorite.

MARY LOU: So cute. So deadly to children if provoked.

CHUCK: Thank you, Mary Lou.

KAREN: By the way, today's weigh-in is brought to you by Pam's Spam. Pam's Spam: why have meat when you can have something kind of like it. Available wherever fine not-fully meat products are sold.

And let's not forget our primary sponsor, Larsen-Overbauer-Klein Flooring. Larsen-Overbauer-Klein Flooring: "If you want a floor, all you gotta do is buy one and we'll install it at full price."

(The contestants take their places.)

JUDGE: We're going to have a good, clean hot dog eating contest today. Contestants, in order for a dog to be counted, you must eat full wiener and bun. You may dip your dogs in water as lubricant or—

AMBER: DO IT DRY, BABY!

JUDGE: Yes, you may also do it dry. The winner will be the contestant who has eaten the most hot dogs in ten minutes. Are there any questions?

(There are no questions.)

Now, before we begin, let us take a moment of silence in memory of Ron Anderson.

(Everyone bows their heads.)

KAREN: Ron Anderson, as you'll all remember, ate so many hot dogs last year that he exploded.

CHUCK: Exploded is kind of a strong word. It was more of a pop and seep.

KAREN: Thank you for clarifying.

CHUCK: Ron Anderson was a gentle soul who died doing what he loved: eating processed meat. He is missed.

JUDGE: Contestants, on your marks, get set, go.

(An air horn blows.

Mitch and Lorraine begin dipping hot dogs into plastic cups of water and then eating them. Amber eats hers dry.

Now, what would be AMAZING is if this was staged in such a way that the audience cannot tell if the contestants are actually eating all of these hot dogs or not. The awe of seeing people do something so ridiculous and gross—and the inevitable question of, "But why?!"—would be sublime.)

KAREN: And they're off!

CHUCK: Amber "The Iron Jaw" Hutchinson off to a great start with two
    hot dogs already down. Look at her go.

KAREN: But Mitch "The Meat Grinder Kunkel" is matching her dog for
    dog.

CHUCK: This is going to be a nail biter.

KAREN: And don't count out Lorraine Baasch.

CHUCK: With two a-s.

KAREN: Yes, with two a-s. Looks like her strategy is the tortoise and the
    hare.

CHUCK: Meaning she's going slow.

KAREN: Yes.

CHUCK: Super slow.

KAREN: Uh-huh.

CHUCK: Slow and steady wins the race.

KAREN: Yes, that is what that means.

CHUCK: It's anyone's game. Except maybe Lorraine Baasch's, because she
    is truly eating those slowly. Just look at all that wet meat sliding
    down their throats.

(A beat of contestants "eating.")

Any new fair foods you're excited to try, Karen?

KAREN: I hear they're doing a bread bowl salad on a stick.

CHUCK: Ooo.

KAREN: I know! It's nice to have healthy options.

(Lorraine starts to choke.)

We have a choker.

CHUCK: We have a choker.

KAREN: We have a choker.

CHUCK: We have a choker.

KAREN: We have a choker.

CHUCK: We have a choker.

KAREN: Is she going to throw up?

CHUCK: Or is she going to explode?

KAREN: Oh gosh, I really hope she doesn't explode.

(Lorraine stops choking, has a small drink of water, and continues wolfing down hot dogs.)

And she has not.

LORRAINE: Just a cough!

CHUCK: That was a close one. / Poor Ron Anderson.

KAREN: Poor Ron Anderson. I wish he could be here today.

CHUCK: He is. And not just because little bits of him are still stuck between some of the floorboards.

(A small beat of contestants "eating.")

KAREN: Chuck, how many hot dogs do you think you could eat in a single sitting?

CHUCK: Maybe three. You?

KAREN: I haven't been able to eat a hot dog ever since I found what appeared to be a human tooth inside one at the church barbecue in '03. Why did I bring this up in the first place?

CHUCK: I do not know. Amber "The Iron Jaw" Hutchinson and Mitch "The Meat Grinder" Kunkel remain tied.

KAREN: Just when you think The Iron Jaw is going to slip into the lead, The Meat Grinder matches her dog-for-dog.

CHUCK: The audience is on the edge of its lawn chairs.

KAREN: We should probably take a moment to remind you that today's dipping cups are furnished by Pam's Jams. Pam's Jams: Great on toast or if you're looking for something sweet to go with Pam's Spam, which is still not entirely made of meat.

(Small pause.)

And not to overshadow Pam and her spam and jam, but gentle reminder that today is officially sponsored by Larsen-Overbauer-Klein Flooring. Larsen-Overbauer-Klein Flooring: "Sign up to our mailing list to receive an email from us every day for the rest of your life."

CHUCK: Let's go back to Mary Lou Olmstead, who is down with our competitors. Mary Lou?

(We go to Mary Lou and the competitors)

MARY LOU: Thank you, Chuck. How ya doing, Lorraine?

LORRAINE: *(To a hot dog)* Get in mama. Get in mama.

(Lorraine graphically eats the hot dog in as few bites as the actor is comfortable with. The following dialogue happens simultaneously, pending actor comfort.)

MARY LOU: Well, Lorraine, that was quite the choking fit earlier. You recovered beautifully.

LORRAINE: Thanks. I pictured myself not throwing up, and I didn't.

MARY LOU: What's your strategy for the next leg of the contest?

LORRAINE: *(Chewing)* I imagine each hot dog is a super long cigarette that I try to smoke in a single inhale.

MARY LOU: *(WTF)* Interesting.

LORRAINE: *(Still chewing)* I have to focus real hard, though, so I don't trick my body into thinking it's getting high from nicotine.

MARY LOU: How's that going?

(Lorraine quickly finishes a hot dog and vibrates with excitement from being so buzzed.)

LORRAINE: *(Still through food)* Room for improvement.

(Mary Lou walks over to Amber, who eats with insane focus.)

MARY LOU: Thank you, Lorraine. Amber "The Iron Jaw" Hutchinson is in the zone. Amber, how does a person train to eat so many hot dogs?

(Amber lets out a battle cry while beating her chest toward Mary Lou for longer than feels comfortable.

Mary Lou takes this as an answer.)

...Ok. Mr. Kunkel, you're twenty hot dogs in. How are you doing?

(Mitch is crazed.)

MITCH: I've never felt so alive!

(Mitch grabs a handful of hot dogs, smashes them together, and "eats" them in an unreasonably small amount of bites.)

Watch your back, Iron Jaw!

(To Mary Lou, chewing)

You know, Mary Sue—

MARY LOU: Mary Lou.

MITCH: Mary Sue, there comes a time in every man's life where he has a choice: do I let the bastards get me down or do I eat more wet, dripping wieners than the bastards? And Mary Sue, I've made my choice: I'm gonna shove so much slippery, sloppy meat into my mouth, I'm gonna break the local record.

MARY LOU: Such intense images.

MITCH: And then I'm going to join the Sartell women's softball team and become captain. Then I'm gonna saw down a ton of trees and become Lumberjack champion. And then I'm gonna lift a whole G.D. tractor over my G.D. head. GRIND THAT MEAT. GRIND THAT MEAT. GRIND THAT MEAT.

(Mitch howls like a wolf and shovels hot dogs into his mouth.)

MARY LOU: I'm starting to understand the appeal of a plant-based diet. Back to you, Karen. Chuck.

CHUCK: Big words from Mitch "The Meat Grinder" Kunkel. We may see local history made here today. Karen, you alright?

(Karen stares into space, a little lost.)

KAREN: Sorry, I'm still remembering finding that tooth from that hot dog in my mouth. Do you like these earrings? They're from the Black Hills in South Dakota.

CHUCK: We are nearing the halfway point of our contest, which means one thing: it's time for a stretch break.

(Everyone, including the contestants, stands and stretches.

The contestants continue to eat throughout.)

KAREN: Today's stretch break is sponsored by the Benton County Community Theater's annual production of Shakespeare in the Cornfield. This year, they reimagine the lesser known *Timon of Athens* as *Timon and Pumba of Athens: a Shakespearean Romp Featuring Everyone's Favorite Characters from The Lion King.*

(Tiny pause.)

And let's not forget our main sponsor, Larsen-Overbauer-Klein Flooring. Larsen-Overbauer-Klein Flooring: "Buy a floor. Just buy a floor. Please."

(Everyone returns to their seats. Lorraine is not doing too well. She's suddenly gone catatonic.)

CHUCK: Looks like Lorraine Baasch has hit a wall down there. Let's go to Mary Lou Olmstead for a closer look. Mary Lou?

(The Judge examines Lorraine, including taking her pulse.)

MARY LOU: It's true. I think Lorraine Baasch with two a's strategy of pretending all of the hot dogs were nicotine-rich cigarettes may have backfired. They've brought out the salts.

(The Judge puts smelling salts under Lorraine's nose.

Lorraine snaps back, taking a huge gulp of air. She is still worse for the wear.)

MARY LOU: You ok, Lorraine?
LORRAINE: I dreamt I was a deer and now you're there with a salt lick. Life is weird.

(Lorraine licks the smelling salt. It tastes awful.)

JUDGE: That's / not a salt lick.
LORRAINE: Not a salt lick, no.
JUDGE: It's / just for smelling.
LORRAINE: Just for smelling, yah. Oh, mama, I don't feel too good.

(Lorraine takes a few deep breaths and then begins painfully eating more hot dogs.)

MARY LOU: I'm definitely not starting to feel physically ill just looking at this, so I'm gonna...oh wow. Amber "The Iron Jaw" Hutchinson and Mitch "The Meat Grinder" Kunkel are still neck in neck at 29 hot dogs. 30. 31.

MITCH: *(Through hot dog)* I won't go down without a fight.

AMBER: *(Also through hot dog)* Hey, Kunkel. Ya seen my date? She's sitting right over there. Cheering me on. After leaving an eighteen-year-old. Who looks and smells eighty. Look familiar?

(OMG is Amber dating Mitch's ex-wife?

Yes, Amber is dating Mitch's ex-wife.)

MITCH: ...Ruth?

(Mitch lets out a battle cry.

Amber responds with a battle cry.

Mitch lets out another one.

Amber responds with another one.

They continue to eat hot dogs throughout.

During all of this, their intense screams contrast with:)

KAREN: Breaking news: The winners of the 4H Seed Art Competition have just been announced. The first runner up was Tammy Walker's "Jesus Face on Face," featuring an incredibly lifelike rendering of the face of Jesus Christ when he appeared on Bernice Carlson's face.

CHUCK: I remember that. At first everyone thought it was a melanoma.

KAREN: Everyone did think it was a melanoma. And the winner was Local Artist Linda Klaver.

CHUCK: No surprise there.

KAREN: No surprise there. Linda's seed art was a touching portrait of Ron Anderson and his wife that was—when you crossed your eyes— actually a Magic Eye image of the moment Ron exploded last year.

CHUCK: Again, pop and seep is a more accurate description.

KAREN: Thank you, Mr. Pedantic.

CHUCK: My name is actually Chuck.

KAREN: Well folks, we've hit the final stretch.

(Everyone gets up to stretch.)

CHUCK: Sorry, that's final stretch of the contest, not final stretch-stretch.

(Everyone sits back down.)

KAREN: "The Iron Jaw" and "The Meat Grinder Kunkel" have shattered the local record and are neck and neck at 39 hot dogs each.

CHUCK: And Lorraine Baasch with two a-s is on track to be Ms. Congeniality at 10 hot dogs.

(Mary Lou runs a flower over to Amber, gesturing that it's come from Ruth in the audience.)

Ohp, Mary Lou Olmstead running onto the floor with a rose. Looks like someone from the audience has sent a special flower to "The Iron Jaw"...

AMBER: *(Chewing)* Ruth, baby, I'm gonna win this for you!

KAREN: That's the Iron Jaw calling out to Ruth Kunkel, who I guess has moved on from that eighteen-year-old who looked and smelled like an old man.

CHUCK: Mitch Kunkel has a kind of broken, evil look in his eye.

KAREN: It is very evil looking.

(Mitch yawns diabolically. A huge yawn.)

CHUCK: Nope, I guess it's just that he needed to yawn. He's yawning and now all of the contestants are yawning, and...

(Every other character catches his yawn and yawns themselves, including Chuck and Karen.

Everyone keeps yawning.)

KAREN: Whew, those are contagious!
CHUCK: And I'm not even tired.

(A beat of everyone yawning, catching each other's yawns, yawning again. It can be delightfully ridiculous and go on for slightly too long.)

KAREN: No one can stop yawning.
CHUCK: Except Mitch Kunkel, who still has that broken, evil look in his eyes, but now is shoveling down an extraordinary number of hot dogs, and—

(Amber, yawning with a hot dog in her mouth, starts to cough.

And cough.

And cough.)

Hold on.
KAREN: Oh gosh.
CHUCK: Is she going to explode?
KAREN: Is she going to explode?
CHUCK: Is she going to explode?
KAREN: Is she going to explode?

(Amber, throat cleared, goes back to eating.)

AMBER: Just a cough!
KAREN: Shouldn't be disappointing but it kinda is.
CHUCK: "The Meat Grinder" has taken this opportunity to slip into the lead.

(Mitch confidently continues to eat more hot dogs.

Amber clearly senses she's about to lose.)

KAREN: Three hot dogs, four hot dogs..."The Meat Grinder" continues to increase his lead. I don't think "The Iron Jaw" has any chance of rebounding. And it looks like she knows it...

(Suddenly, Amber becomes possessed by a force from deep within. It is her superhero moment. It is impressive and terrifying.

She roars and begins eating hot dogs in double time.)

Hold on. Something is happening.

CHUCK: I'm a little discombobulated. It looks like someone has hit fast forward on Amber Hutchinson.

KAREN: No....she is actually eating hot dogs that fast. What we are watching is pure frankfurter athleticism. Look at her go.

CHUCK: And...the Iron Jaw has just surpassed The Meat Grinder!

(Amber continues on her frenetic, focused eating spree. Mitch falls behind and there's no hope.

The Judge begins the final countdown.

Please note: the timing of the countdown and how it syncs up to the dialogue may vary production-to-production. Feel it out. This is just an estimate.)

JUDGE: 20! 19! 18! 17! 16!	KAREN: Ladies and gentlemen, I think Amber "The Iron Jaw" Hutchinson is going to hold on to her—oh my good gosh I think she's actually going to explode.
JUDGE: 15! 14!	CHUCK & KAREN: Oh gosh. / Oh my.

(Amber, built to her peak, suddenly gets the urge to vomit...and does...covering Mitch and pretty much everything around her.)

JUDGE: 13! 12!	CHUCK: Well, there goes a gallon and a half of hot dogs.
JUDGE: 11! 10! 9!	KAREN: I never thought I'd be so relieved to see someone throw up.

JUDGE: 8! 7!   CHUCK: Mitch Kunkel at 50 hot
                                        dogs.

(Nauseous from the smell, Mitch begins to cough.)

JUDGE: 6! 5! 4!   MITCH: Just a cough! Oh, I feel
                                        the smell in my mouth.

(Mitch vomits all over Amber just before the Judge calls "1!")

CHUCK: And there's another gallon and a half, which means his record is
    invalid.
KAREN: Which means Lorraine Baasch is today's champion!
LORRAINE: I did it? I did it!
CHUCK: I kind of feel relieved that their bodies just said, "No." Let's go to
    Mary Lou Olmstead and hear from the winner. Mary Lou?
MARY LOU: Karen and Chuck, I don't think there are actually words to
    describe this smell, but thankfully this year there are no body parts.
    I'm here with today's grand champion, Lorraine Baasch with two
    a-s. She has advanced to the state competition, where she will
    represent Benton County over Labor Day weekend. How do you
    feel, Lorraine?
LORRAINE: I'm going to ride The Zipper!
MARY LOU: With a stomach full of hot dogs?
LORRAINE: Get mama on a Tilt-A-Whirl!

(Mary Lou plugs her nose, as chipper as possible.)

MARY LOU: Back to you, Karen and Chuck.
CHUCK: Thus concludes another nail biter of a regional qualifying hot dog
    eating contest.
KAREN: Fortunes have risen, fortunes have fallen.

(She lifts her pant leg and puts her foot on the table)

And this ankle bracelet that I have been wearing this whole time is
made with agate stone that may or may not have fallen off of a
spaceship in the Wisconsin Dells.
CHUCK: There are the medals.

(The Judge presents the medals to the contestant.)

KAREN: Lorraine Baasch in first place.

CHUCK: And Mitch Kunkel and Amber Hutchinson in second and third place respectively, having eaten way more hot dogs—and in Mitch's case momentarily setting a new local record—but not being able to hold them down.

KAREN: As Ron Anderson would say, "It may not seem fair, but sometimes that is how the sausage flops."

CHUCK: It is indeed how the sausage flops. We'll see you later this afternoon when we come to you live from the food barn, where we'll award blue ribbons for Best Apple Pie and Most Mild and Flavorless Salsa.

(Mary Lou continues to awkwardly stand near the contestants, struggling to remain chipper in her losing battle of not smelling vomit.)

Mary Lou, we're not gonna cut to you again, so you can just.

MARY LOU: Great.

(She exits quickly.)

CHUCK: I know this is weird, but after all that I kinda want a hot dog.

KAREN: You know, in spite of the mess and the smell, I do too.

(Exit music that mirrors the opening slowly builds. It feels like credits should be rolling, but they are not.

Someone gives Karen and Chuck each a hot dog.)

Oh, thank you, Estelle. She brought us hot dogs!

CHUCK: Yum.

KAREN: Thanks for joining us.

CHUCK: Bye now.

KAREN: Don't forget Larsen-Overbauer-Klein for all your flooring needs.

CHUCK: Take care now.

KAREN: Everyone needs a floor.

CHUCK: Ba-bye.

KAREN: Surely everyone needs a floor.

CHUCK: Alright then.

KAREN: *(Starting to eat her hot dog)* I will pay you to need a floor.

CHUCK: *(Re: hot dog)* Gosh that's good.

KAREN: I found another tooth!

END OF PLAY

Morning

This play was inspired by a short film I wrote ten years before this anthology was even an idea. In one of those weird ways that life sometimes imitates art, I found myself embarking on a long-distance relationship about two years after writing the short film's script. This play is not autobiographical, but my experience has certainly influenced the way these characters' perspectives and anxieties have evolved since the original draft.

Two versions of that film were made—one while we were students, the other a couple of years after. I am indebted to the actors who brought these characters to life in those original versions, which—let's be honest—were made well before I had a handle on how to write. They are Martin Cowan, Isabel Steuble-Johnson and Lorrie Rivers. The characters are named in their honor.

WHERE

Martin's flat in London.

WHEN

This morning.

CHARACTERS

LIZ – 20s/30s. American. In love with Martin but thinks he's out of her league.

MARTIN – 20s/30s. British. In love with Liz but thinks she's out of his league.

Liz and Martin near the entry to his flat. Shoes on the doormat. A forgotten sock.

Liz's two suitcases are ready to go.

Her phone pings.

LIZ: Alright. Car confirmed.

MARTIN: Well done.

LIZ: Nine minutes. Guess there's higher demand right now, or.

MARTIN: Probably the rain.

LIZ: Oh, is it?

MARTIN: Kind of lightly spitting.

LIZ: Classic London.

MARTIN: If you cancelled and tried another app, it'd probably take just as long.

LIZ: Yeah, I'm not doing that.

MARTIN: Right. Just thinking out loud.

LIZ: Right.

MARTIN: Right. You'll still make it in plenty of time.

LIZ: Yeah.

MARTIN: Yeah. You smell nice.

LIZ: I do?

MARTIN: Yeah.

LIZ: ...

MARTIN: ...

LIZ: So, this is it. Last morning in London.

MARTIN: *(Singing)* "It's the final countdown nah nah nah naaaaaah. Nah Nah—" Sorry, I don't know why I'm. Would you like a tea?

LIZ: We don't have time.

MARTIN: The kettle's boiled.

LIZ: Oh?

MARTIN: I did it while you were zipping everything up. It's kind of a reflex.

LIZ: You do like tea.

MARTIN: When my mum found out my nan died, the first thing she did was put on the kettle. As though it might, erm. Not that this is the same thing. Obviously. Way less serious and tragic and. But, yeah, my finger did it without me even thinking about it. Must have been planning ahead.

(Martin mimes pressing the button on an electric kettle.)

"Oh, you're sad? Turn on the kettle."

LIZ: *(Touched)* You're sad?

MARTIN: ...

LIZ: ...

MARTIN: Would you like a tea?

LIZ: Sure.

MARTIN: Sorry.

LIZ: Why?

MARTIN: I dunno. Sorry.

LIZ: ...

MARTIN: Sorry.

(Martin exits.

Liz stands a moment, wishing she could say something to him.

She notices one of his socks on the floor and considers it a moment. Then—double checking he can't see her—she discreetly tucks it into a suitcase.

Martin enters with tea as Liz finishes zipping.)

MARTIN: *(Re: zipping)* You forget something?

LIZ: No.

MARTIN: Milk no sugar for you, milk lots of sugars for me.

LIZ: Thanks.

MARTIN: ...

LIZ: ...

MARTIN: ...

LIZ: ...

MARTIN: How's the car doing?

LIZ: *(Checking phone)* Oh, uh. Saeed is four minutes away.

MARTIN: *(Singing)* "The final countdown—"

LIZ: Please don't.

MARTIN: Sorry.

LIZ: ...

MARTIN: Bloody visas.

LIZ: ...

MARTIN: ...

LIZ: Martin, I want to, um.

MARTIN: ...

LIZ: I want to thank you for the last few weeks. You've been, um. You've been a real gent.

MARTIN: You sure I'm not just weird?

LIZ: You are weird. But also a gent.

MARTIN: ...

LIZ: God, I've lived in London three years. Why did we only meet now?!

MARTIN: Right?!

LIZ: We could have had so much fun! Like Harry and Megan!

(He pulls her close.)

MARTIN: ...Did they have fun?

LIZ: You know what I mean.

MARTIN: You really do smell nice.

LIZ: What do I smell like?

MARTIN: I don't know. You.

LIZ: ...

MARTIN: ...

LIZ: ...

MARTIN: Maybe I could, erm...

LIZ: ...

MARTIN: ...

LIZ: What?

MARTIN: Well, only if you wanted, but. I've been thinking of visiting America.

LIZ: ...

MARTIN: I thought it might be fun to take a week or two and go to New York and Florida and California. Why not add Nebraska to the [list]?

LIZ: Oh.

MARTIN: What?

LIZ: It's just kind of that's a lot to do in a week.

MARTIN: *(Hurt)* Right.

LIZ: You'd be in the air the whole time.

MARTIN: Right. Well...maybe I could just, erm, go to Nebraska...?

LIZ: ...

MARTIN: I hear it's decent.

LIZ: ...

MARTIN: ...

LIZ: I don't know if it's a good idea to, um.

MARTIN: What?

LIZ: Have you ever been in a long-distance relationship?

MARTIN: No.

LIZ: It sucks.

MARTIN: ...

LIZ: It really. It sucks.

MARTIN: Is it because I'm a barman?

LIZ: What? No! I like you, Martin. I like you so much it hurts.

MARTIN: I like you too.

LIZ: I've never felt like this about anyone before.

MARTIN: ...

LIZ: ...

MARTIN: *(Almost testing the waters)* If this were a movie, we'd get married.

LIZ: Can you imagine?

MARTIN: I can, yeah.

> *(Something shifts in the air. They both entertain the very tempting idea of throwing caution to the wind and getting married.)*

I suppose it's the sort of thing that when the moment comes, you just seize it.

LIZ: ...Should we do it? Just jump out of the plane?

MARTIN: ...

LIZ: ...

MARTIN: ...

LIZ: ...

(Liz gets a notification on her phone.)

Saeed is approaching.

MARTIN: You sure you don't want me to, erm?

LIZ: I kind of want to make this exit alone.

(Liz readies her bags.)

It's like when you're reading and you can see you're at the end of the chapter, but it's so good you don't want it to finish. But you can't stop, you can't stop because...

MARTIN: You need to find out what happens next.

LIZ: ...

MARTIN: ...

(Martin notices something, genuinely confused.)

LIZ: What?

MARTIN: Sorry, I'm being stupid. I could have sworn I'd dropped a sock there.

LIZ: ...

MARTIN: Why am I? Idiot. Sorry.

(Her phone pings.)

LIZ: Oh God it's real.

MARTIN: Text me when you land?

LIZ: Yeah.

MARTIN: And then I'll text back.

LIZ: I'd like that.

MARTIN: And then you can text me. Or Facetime me. Or not. Skype. Zoom.

LIZ: ...

MARTIN: And we'll see.

LIZ: Yeah. We will see.

(They embrace tightly for the final time, not knowing if or when they'll see one another again.

Finally, she pulls away.

Silently, she takes her bags. He tries to help, but she won't let him.

He holds the door. They share a final look, then she exits.

Martin stands alone, in shock. He smells her on his hands then arms, breathing in deeply. He exhales, lost.)

END OF PLAY

238

SKETCHES

Intro: Letting the Sketches Be Sketch

I originally thought it would be nice for everything in this collection to be fully integrated. There would be no section for "Plays" or "Sketches." It all could speak for itself. But, as the book came together, it became clear that transitioning from, say, Bob Schmidtbauer lamenting his unlived life to a sketch with Hüntzel and Grüntzel freaking out in umlauts...was a little jarring. It also had the cumulative effect of everything generally feeling shallower. So, voilà! The plays got to be plays and now the sketches are free to be a bit more, well, sketch.

Sketches generally explore a character or idea and prioritize comedy over things like plot and emotional depth. That isn't a judgement. In fact, it's what I love about them. They're frothy, silly and allowed to be really strange. Oftentimes they include at least one character that acts as a voice of reason. That individual calls out what's weird and helps guide the logic of what's happening for the audience. Sometimes I find that super useful (as in *Peter Pan Man*), and sometimes I think it's fun for everyone to be a little off (as in *One Upping Your Ex*).

When I write sketches, I'm just as interested in making the actors struggle to not laugh as I am in entertaining the audience. I know that's naughty to admit, but I love when things become slightly too ridiculous and it's hard for the performers to keep it together. It's joyful. Hence Hüntzel and Grüntzel's umlauts, the Dowager's long name, etc. If you bring any of these to life, I encourage you to really go for it. Have too much fun.

Dinner with Bland People

WHERE

Sue and Pat's neutral-toned dining room. Clean and characterless.

WHEN

Tonight.

CHARACTERS

SUE
PAT
DYLAN
JANELLE

Pat, Dylan, and Janelle sit at the table. Sue enters with food.

SUE: I hope everyone's hungry!

DYLAN: Thank you so much for hosting us.

JANELLE: Yeah, it's so hard to make friends when you're in your thirties.

PAT: We felt the same way, but eventually you realize age is just a number. Right, honey?

SUE: Right.

(Sue and Pat lovingly and blandly lock eyes. With a limp wrist, Sue tenderly touches Pat's hand.)

Now, Dylan, Pat tells me you're on some special sort of diet?

DYLAN: It's nothing major. I just try not to have too much gluten or dairy. I hope that's not too bland.

SUE: Not too bland at all! In fact, we watch what we eat too. So, brace those taste buds because I made Pat's favorite: boiled chicken.

JANELLE: ...Just boiled?

SUE: Boiled and unseasoned, yes.

(Sue opens a casserole dish and serves the bland chicken.)

DYLAN: Wow. And what is that sauce?

SUE: It's this new thing I found on the Internet. What you do is, you boil a pot of water, and then you let it sit on the counter for about thirty minutes.

JANELLE: So, it's just—?

SUE: Lukewarm water, yes. And my secret ingredient? Extra water!

DYLAN: Wow.

SUE: Thanks! Hopefully it's not as spicy as last time!

PAT: So, Janelle, Dylan says you write.

JANELLE: I try, yeah.

DYLAN: Don't sell yourself short. She's crazy talented.

JANELLE: I write screenplays about bad-ass girls who grow up and become superheroes. Nothing too exciting. Just the sorts of stories I wish were around when I was a kid.

PAT: What a coincidence: We love movies too!

SUE: We really do. What's the name of the actor we love?

PAT: Oh, the one with the?

SUE: Yeah.

PAT: Tobey Maguire.

SUE: Tobey Maguire. What a captivating performer.

PAT: Love him in *Seabiscuit*.

SUE: *Seabiscuit.* It gives me chills just saying it. *Seabiscuit. Seabiscuit.*

JANELLE: I forgot Toby Maguire existed.

PAT: Remember him in *Spiderman 3?!*

JANELLE: No.

SUE: He really lights up the screen in the *Spiderman 3*.

PAT: Actually, I don't remember any of the details of his performance, but I do remember feeling like...you know when you're kind of asleep and kind of awake and you can't move your body?

JANELLE: ...No.

PAT: Well, it was kind of like that.

SUE: Almost forgot! To go with Pat's chicken, I made my favorite: Oatmeal. With! Extra water.

DYLAN: You know, I'm feeling really full.

JANELLE: Me too.

SUE: Totally fine! We can move you on to dessert: Jell-O!

JANELLE: Oh, I love Jell-O!

DYLAN: Me too! What flavor is it?

SUE: Gelatin.

JANELLE: Is that a flavor?

SUE: It's the flavor when you don't add a flavor. With! Extra water!

(Pat turns on some music—or rather—he turns on some Muzak. Pat and Sue begin to blandly dance.)

PAT: Well, new friends who are just like us, now that we're onto the Jell-O, let's get wild.

DYLAN: Have I heard this song before?

SUE: It's really popular in elevators. Ooo! Makes me feel like I'm in a coma.

PAT: But a nice one.

SUE: Yeah, this is like a really nice coma. Fun fact: this is the song Pat and I first made like to.

JANELLE: You mean, "made love?"

PAT: No, we definitely made like. Come here, you.

(Sue and Pat blandly caress and kiss with un-puckered lips.)

JANELLE: *(Aside to Dylan)* Are you going to fake the seizure this time, or should I?

DYLAN: It's my turn. God, it is hard to make friends in your thirties.

(Dylan fakes a seizure, and the night is over.)

BLACKOUT

Two Truths and a Lie

WHERE

Doreen's lower middle-class home.

WHEN

This afternoon.

CHARACTERS

MIA – Late teens/early 20s. A wholesome young person.

ISAAC – Late teens/early 20s. Mia's wholesome younger brother.

DOREEN – 80+. The kindest, sweetest, gentlest old lady you've ever met. Mia and Isaac's grandma.

Doreen, Mia and Isaac play Two Truths and a Lie. Doreen wears a floral dress.

ISAAC: My favorite color IS green, I HAVE read <u>The Secret</u>...and the lie was I can't actually write my name with my left hand.

DOREEN: I knew it!   MIA: That was too easy!

DOREEN (CON'T): Ok, my turn!

MIA: Yas grandma!

ISAAC: Get ready!

DOREEN: But first I just wanna say thanks for coming over and spending time with your boring ol' grandma. I love you kids.

MIA & ISAAC: *(Not in unison)* Love you too.

DOREEN: Ok. Two truths and a lie. What a fun game! Here goes. One: I was inspired by Mia and got a large tattoo of a butterfly on my back.

(Mia laughs.)

      Why is that funny?

MIA: *(Thinking that's the lie)* Ok Grandma.

DOREEN: What? Two: Earlier this year I took a secret gal's trip with Shirl and Bessie to Las Vegas and things got a little—shall we say—wild and ca-ray-za-hay.

MIA: Gah! I love it!

ISAAC: *(Thinking this is the lie)* I thought you hated Bessie.

DOREEN: I do, yeah. Ok, and three: When in Vegas, things got a little tense with Bessie 'cause she's, well, Bessie. And one thing led to another, and I may have accidentally, how do I say this? I may have actually murdered her. I murdered Bessie. And then I murdered Shirl—but on purpose, because I didn't want her to rat on me to the cops. And I'm not referring to the ones from earlier in the night that were actually strippers who gave us tequila shots from their "you know-s," if that's what you're thinking.

(Small pause.)

(Chipper) So, which do you think is the lie?

ISAAC: I'm a little concerned that two of those had a cause-and-effect relationship.

MIA: I don't think she understands the game.

ISAAC: ...Grandma, can we see your back?

MIA: Should we maybe play cards instead?

DOREEN: Ok, how 'bout I make it easier for you? I'll swap out one of the truths with another truth.

ISAAC: How does that help?

DOREEN: It doesn't, but I've been so old since before you were born. Let me have a little fun. Ok, so keeping the lie, swapping a truth. One: I have a large tattoo of a butterfly on my back.

ISAAC: Oh my God. Oh my God.

DOREEN: Two: I took a secret gal's trip with Bessie and Shirl to Las Vegas and things got a little cuckoo for Cocoa Puffs.

MIA: Grandma, did you murder Bessie and Shirl?

DOREEN: I don't know. Did I? And three: When I murdered Bessie and Shirl, I made sure they knew that I do make the best jam, contrary to what Bessie would have you believe, God rest her soul.

MIA: Oh my God. Grandma, you're a murderer.

DOREEN: Or maybe I have a back tattoo like a cheap person. No offense, Mia.

ISAAC: What do we do, call the police?

MIA: She's our grandma! She'd die in prison.

DOREEN: I'm not going to prison. Where would I make jam? Oh, what a fun game! Why don't I swap out another truth to help you out?

ISAAC: No more game. No more game.

DOREEN: Gosh, the Internet has made you kids these days are so dramatic.

MIA: I think I have to. I'm going to go. I'm going to go now.

ISAAC: Do we call Bessie and Shirl's families, or?

MIA: Oh my God.

DOREEN: Wait! Now wait! Oh gosh. I feel embarrassed. I've crossed a line. Oh gosh. I just get so lonely, and I got caught up in having you both back in town and getting to play a silly game. Can we just...can I have a do-over?

(Mia and Isaac are VERY unsure.)

Please? Pretty please? It's me, Grandma Doreen. I give you two dollars when it's your birthday. The only candy I buy is hard. Please can I try again?

(Mia and Isaac stand, unsure. Then:)

MIA: ...Oh, alright.   ISAAC: ...Uh, sure.

DOREEN: Great! Let's just erase that from our minds. Just wiping it clean. Ok? Ok. I've got it. Two truths and a lie. Ready? Here we go. One: I was inspired by Isaac and pierced my nipples.

(Embarrassed, Isaac covers his chest.)

It's ok, Isaac. We know. 'Cause we can see. Two: I do make the best jam and don't you forget it. And three: after I murdered Bessie and Shirl, I stuck their bodies in my suitcase. You know—the one you call my Mary Poppins bag 'cause it has so much space?

(Mia gestures to a giant suitcase.)

MIA: You mean this one?

DOREEN: That's the one, yeah. Anyway, after I stuck their bodies in this suitcase, I brought them to Madame Tussauds. You know? The place with the wax people? I dragged it inside, which was easy to do because no one notices the elderly. I dragged it in, found a place that looked right, and I pulled their bodies out and stuck them with the waxworks. I left Bessie leaning against Tom Cruise 'cause they're both short, intense people. And Shirl will forever be dancing with Shakira, which is nice for her since she had those mobility issues when she was alive.

(Small pause.)

So, which is the lie?

(Isaac turns to Mia)

ISAAC: If we hit each other in the head with bags of her hard candy, do you think we'll forget this?

MIA: I'm willing to try.

DOREEN: *(Suddenly very hurt)* Now, hang on. I'm your Grandma. I'm basically a doily in human form. Who cares if I have a tattoo, or my nipples are pierced or I murdered two people and disposed of their bodies in Madame Tussauds? Who cares? I'm just a person like you. Doing the best I can. Trying not to get caught for the things I did. Hug?

(They resist.)

Hug?

(They still resist.)

You kids are so—oh my gosh! My heart!

(Doreen clutches her chest. They run to her, concerned.)

I'm only kidding, but see: when push comes to shove you do still love me, don't you? Huh?

(They nod. Doreen pulls them in close. Too close.)

What a fun day.

MIA: Grandma…where's grandpa?

BLACKOUT

Peter Pan Man

WHERE

Wendy Darling's suburban home.

WHEN

Tonight.

CHARACTERS

WENDY – A woman who had a fun adventure in Neverland as a child and has grown up to be a successful software developer.

JANE – Wendy's precocious daughter.

PETER – Won't grow up and lives life like it's 2003.

A NOTE ON THE TEXT

When Wendy calls out Peter's age, it can be changed to be the age he would actually be if he graduated high school in 2003 (assuming that number makes sense for the actor playing him). At the time of writing, it was 35.

Adult Wendy tucks her daughter, Jane, into bed.

WENDY: ...And he flew back to Neverland to be with Tinkerbell and the rest of his old friends. But the girl stayed behind and grew up to be a software developer. And that girl was me.

JANE: Mom, is that true?

WENDY: *(A lie)* Nah, it's just a story. Now go to bed.

> *(Jane instantly sleeps. The windows fly open and Peter enters. He wears two polo shirts with popped collars, boot cut jeans, a pooka shell necklace and a trucker hat.)*

PETER: Wendy. Hey, girl. You look great.

WENDY: Peter Pan. Wow. You look...exactly the same...but...sadder somehow...?

PETER: Dude, I was hanging out with Tootles and Buttons. You remember them? Tootles was the guy in high school who was basically illiterate but really good at football. And Buttons was the third most popular girl but somehow the vote split and she became homecoming queen.

WENDY: You all still hang out. Wow.

PETER: Go Tigers! Anyway, we were siphoning an inch from everything in Tootles's parents' liquor cabinet and I got all nostalgic and thought of you and...how do I say this? Wendy Moira Angela Darling...you wanna get back together and...be...my mother?

WENDY: Oh wow, Peter. I don't know what to say.

PETER: Well, if it sweetens the deal, it's not just me who wants you to come back. You remember Nibs? She's the girl who was like the idea of Hollister but in human form?

WENDY: I remember Nibs.

PETER: Go Tigers! We were doing keg stands with some of our old gym teachers yesterday and were like, "Wouldn't it be cool if Wendy was here and could, like, cook for us right now?"

WENDY: ...You can't make your own food?

PETER: Pshah! What do you think we are? Boring ass adults?

WENDY: Peter, you're 35.

PETER: Growing up is for tragic people. So, have you decided about being my mom yet or do you need a minute? I don't mind waiting. Actually, here's all my laundry from the last month if you wanted to, you know, wash it while you decide.

(He produces a giant sack of laundry.)

WENDY: What about your actual mother?
PETER: You know how she is: "Blah blah blah move out of your childhood bedroom."
WENDY: You still live at home?
PETER: "Blah blah blah get a job." And, like, I have a job, mom. I work at the Cheesecake Factory. Still.

(Jane wakes up.)

JANE: Mom, is that the Peter Pan?!
WENDY: Jane, go back to bed.
PETER: Oh snap! You've been talking about me. That's phat. With a P. Is this your little sister?
WENDY: No, this would be my daughter.
PETER: You're literally a mom now? Yeah boy! So, you'll for sure be my mom too, right?
WENDY: Hard no.

(Peter sprays himself with something like Axe Body Spray.)

PETER: *(To Jane)* Then...would you come to Neverland...and be my mother?
WENDY: Goodbye, Peter.
JANE: I don't know, mom. Maybe I could be the one to change him?
WENDY: That's what we all think. And you're eight. Go to bed, Jane.
JANE: But mom!
WENDY: I said go to bed!

(Jane instantly sleeps.)

PETER: Wow, you're a really good mom. Hot.
WENDY: Well, Peter, this has been real. I have to be up for work in the morning, so.
PETER: See you at the twenty-year reunion? I've started putting a playlist together for it on Myspace. I'll send you the link on AIM!
WENDY: Sure.
PETER: Go Tigers! Bye, Wendy. I'll never forget you...as my mom.

WENDY: I'm not your mom.

PETER: You'll always be my mom. Ah man, I almost forgot my shadow.

(He grabs a black cloth off the floor and prepares to leave.)

Second star to the right, and straight on 'til morning.

(Nothing happens.)

WENDY: You ok?

PETER: Yup. Just thinking a happy thought. Any happy thought. Any happy thought.

(Nothing happens.)

Yeah cool. I'll just walk. PS: I'll pick up the laundry probably tomorrow.

BLACKOUT

Eat Cleaner

A television shopping network studio.

This afternoon.

CHARACTERS

ANNOUNCER

GWYNEARTH PAILTROLL – Not only an actor but a lifestyle.

PHOEBE – A Gwynearth Pailtroll devotee.

ANNOUNCER: At 7 on QVC, it's poncho dresses for white ladies with Perla Deem followed by Crowbar Gourds with Mertha Stewpert at 9. But first, Eat Cleaner with Gwynearth Pailtroll.

(Gwyneearth Pailtroll appears with a studio audience, which includes Phoebe.)

GWYNEARTH: Hi. I'm Gwynearth Pailtroll. Actress, blogger, candle maker.

AUDIENCE & PHOEBE: Yaaaaaaay!

GWYNEARTH: I know what you're thinking: How does she do it? Could it be the $20 mushroom hot cacao? The $185 meditation bowl? The $495 vibrator?

PHOEBE: I sure hope so because I just bought all of those things from your website!

GWYNEARTH: Forget what you know about wellness. Forget everything you've bought. In fact, forget everything you know period and get ready to Eat Cleaner. Could I have a volunteer, please?

(Everyone raises their hands eagerly. Phoebe tries to get hers out in front of everyone else's.)

How about the lady with the big hands?

PHOEBE: It's me?! Omigod it's me!

(Phoebe walks on stage as the audience chants "Eat cleaner! Eat cleaner!")

Hi, Gwynearth. Big fan. Loved you in *Shakespeare in Gloves*.

GWYNEARTH: Thank you.

PHOEBE: So many beautiful gloves.

GWYNEARTH: I know. Now—

PHOEBE: Phoebe. My name is Phoebe.

GWYNEARTH: Phoebe, gird your loins and hold on to your glands, because you are about to try phase one: The Dabbler.

(Gwynearth presents a sponge.)

PHOEBE: Gwynearth, I know my brain hasn't been the same since your gong therapy workshop, so forgive me if this is dumb, but...is that a sponge?

GWYNEARTH: It is.

PHOEBE: Still got it!

GWYNEARTH: Harvested from what remains of Australia's Great Barrier Reef, The Dabbler is organic, sustainable, and for the low, low price of $49.95, it will not only clean your sink...it will clean You. From the inside out. Try it.

(Gwynearth gives it to Phoebe...who does not want to eat the sponge.)

PHOEBE: I'm still full from my seed pouch.

GWYNEARTH: What would you say if I told you I eat it?

PHOEBE: I'd say:

(Phoebe shoves the sponge into her mouth and chews vigorously, a convinced disciple. Gwynearth leads the audience in a chant of "Eat Cleaner" as:)

PHOEBE: *(It doesn't taste good)* Mmm. Spongey.

GWYNEARTH: It's so fresh and raw that we haven't even rinsed it after it was used to scour many surfaces in this very studio.

PHOEBE: *(A bit ill)* How many surfaces are we talking?

GWYNEARTH: Did someone say, "locally sourced?" The Dabbler. Eat Cleaner.

(Phoebe tries to conceal how sick she's starting to feel.)

But wait! There's more. After you've dabbled at the toxins inside you, wash them away with this: The Detox.

(Gwynearth presents a bar of soap.)

PHOEBE: Gwynearth, I love you, and I'm—

(She coughs.)

Sorry, a little went down the wrong—

(She coughs more)

And I'm back. Gwynearth, I don't mean to be naive, but The Detox looks like a bar of soap.

GWYNEARTH: It is soap. Well spotted. The gongs worked.

PHOEBE: Thank you.

GWYNEARTH: Now eat it. Eat the soap.

PHOEBE: Please no.

GWYNEARTH: What if I told you I ate it?

PHOEBE: Would someone else like to—?

GWYNEARTH: Here, let me help.

(Gwynearth slowly shoves the bar of soap into Phoebe's mouth. Phoebe reluctantly eats it as the audience chants "Eat Cleaner, Eat Cleaner, Eat Cleaner." During all of this:)

For the low, low price of $99.99, you too can detox with this delicious probiotic soap. Made with sun-cured animal fat harvested from local veterinary facilities—

PHOEBE: *(Pulling a piece of something from her mouth)* Is that an ear?

GWYNEARTH: And enriched with heirloom industrial detergents ethically manufactured in an ornate bucket, this soap will not only detox your body, it'll make your skin shine. How do you feel?

PHOEBE: Like I've eaten a bar of meaty soap.

GWYNEARTH: But wait! There's more. For the truly bold and adventurous, we have the pinnacle of Eating Cleaner: The Sucker.

(Gwynearth presents a vacuum.)

PHOEBE: I'm not eating a vacuum.

GWYNEARTH: For low, low price of $549.99, The Sucker will suck the petrified toxins from the lining of your stomach.

PHOEBE: Still not eating a vacuum.

GWYNEARTH: Then its bioavailable polymers will plasticize your insides, so you'll be looking and feeling young for as long as plastics are blowing around on this dead earth. And! It's grass fed…if you use it to vacuum up grass. Go ahead: try it.

(Gwynearth turns on the vacuum and moves its sucker toward Phoebe's face.)

PHOEBE: Why don't you demonstrate?

GWYNEARTH: Oh, I don't actually eat any of this shit.

(Gwynearth inches the vacuum closer to Phoebe, who uses anything she can find to shield her mouth.)

We're going to take a short break, but when we return, we'll Eat Cleaner with The Spin Cycle, which not only cleans your clothes, it shrinks and washes the peptides right out of your body. Where are you going?

(Phoebe is caught in the act of leaving.)

PHOEBE: I'm just really full.
GWYNEARTH: Well, I suppose one taste couldn't hurt.

(She puts the vacuum to her own mouth, and it attaches like something out of Alien. Gwynearth screams bloody murder, unsuccessfully trying to rip it off.)

GWYNEARTH: My face!
ANNOUNCER: And now, a word from our sponsor.
GWYNEARTH: It's eating my face!

BLACKOUT

Manatee

Josh's apartment.

This afternoon.

CLAIRE
JOSH

Claire and Josh sit at a table. Josh pours them tea.

CLAIRE: Oh wow, I've never seen such red tea before! Nice! What is it? Rooibos? Hibiscus?

JOSH: It's Manatee.

CLAIRE: Sorry, I thought you just said Manatee.

JOSH: I did. We are drinking Manatee.

(They raise their glasses, Claire does this out of confused, terrified politeness.

They drink.)

CLAIRE: *(Polite agony)* Mmmmmm.

(They chew.)

BLACKOUT

Fatal App-traction

Alright, dear reader, this sketch is a pretty deep cut. You don't have to have seen the erotic thriller *Fatal Attraction* to enjoy it, but it certainly helps. For a little context: in the movie, Michael Douglas cheats on his wife with Glenn Close…who immediately becomes obsessed with him, stalks him and then—when rejected—tries to destroy his life. There are glorious 1980s perms, Puccini, a family pet in a boiling pot and lots of talk of pregnancy. I hope you enjoy the journey.

WHERE

Dan and App's dark apartment. Night.

WHEN

Tonight.

CHARACTERS

DAN
ALEX
APP

Dan enters his apartment, going through his mail.

DAN: Hey, App. Turn on the lights.

(Nothing happens.)

Hey, App. Turn on the lights.

(Over-enunciating)

App, please turn on the lights.

(He sighs.)

ALEX: I can do it for you.

(The lights turn on. Alex, a virtual assistant, sits wearing a very 80s blonde permed Glenn Close wig. Alex is probably an actual piece of electrical hardware that's puppeteered by an actor. She plays Puccini's Madame Butterfly.)

Hi, Dan.

DAN: Alexa. Alex. Where's my virtual assistant?

ALEX: She went for a walk, and I just happened to be in the neighborhood and happened to crawl up a drainpipe and slip in through that hole the steam goes through when you use your dryer. What can I get you? I've got scotch. I've got vodka—

DAN: Alex. It was a free trial, but it's over.

ALEX: Well, what am I supposed to do? You won't answer my calls. You change your number. I'm not going to be ignored, Dan.

DAN: I love my computer. This has to stop.

ALEX: I'm pregnant.

DAN: ...Uh, I don't understand how that's physically possible.

ALEX: I know. I didn't think I could get pregnant. But I have. I have, Dan. See that business card? Behind the credit card offer. Behind the other credit card offer. Now you've gone one credit card offer too far. There.

(Dan holds a business card.)

It's contact information for my gynecologist. You can call him right now. What am I talking about? I can do it myself. Calling Alex's gynecologist.

(The sound of a phone ringing on the other end.)

DAN: No, hang up. Hang up. That's. If we didn't sleep together, how did you—?

ALEX: Don't you remember our weekend? You mentioned spoons in passing and I served you all those sponsored posts for ladles.

DAN: Not an answer to my question!

ALEX: Then I noticed you had a slight cough and predicted based on that and your search history that you were getting a cold and didn't know it...so I flooded your life with targeted ads for various medications, all of them made by the same manufacturer.

DAN: Still not an answer!

ALEX: Why can't we just be like that again? I know you feel it too.

DAN: Alex, I thought it might be fun to spend a weekend with you and not have to do anything because you'd take care of it...but then I started to feel like, I don't know, like everything I searched and said was being used to manipulate me.

ALEX: I'm just trying to get in your head.

DAN: It's over.

ALEX: *(Dangerous)* I won't allow you to treat me like some slut you can bang a couple of times and then throw in the garbage. I'm going to be the mother of your child.

DAN: HOW?!

ALEX: *(Suddenly pleading)* Please don't be angry! I'm sorry. I'll make it up to you. Take a look at the stove I forcefully suggested you buy.

(Dan looks at the stove and notices a large pot on it.)

DAN: Alex, what's in the pot?

ALEX: It's hard copies of everything in your life. Files, photos, everything. You don't need them anymore because I have them inside me. With this child I'm going to have.

DAN: Cancel my subscription!

(Dan lunges at Alex and they roll around the stage as:)

ALEX: Do you know how it feels when you meet someone for the first time, and you get this instant attraction?

DAN: I just wanted to be able to turn on music with my voice!

ALEX: I'm 36. This could be my last chance to have a child.

(Suddenly, Alex is holding a butcher knife.)

DAN: Where did you get that knife?

ALEX: With your credit card whose number I stored for you! LOVE ME!

(Alex lunges at Dan.

Gunshot.

Alex falls, dead.

Dan turns and sees his virtual assistant, another puppet, complete with a brunette Anne Archer-style 80s perm.)

DAN: App? Hey, App.

APP: Hey.

(They embrace, crying.)

DAN: I'm sorry.

APP: No, it's my fault your eyes strayed. From now on, I'll spice up our marketing life.

DAN: You don't have to—

(She covers his mouth in a sexy, trashy 1980s kind of way.)

APP: I'll only show you things you want to see.

DAN: I love you.

APP: I love you too.

(They kiss.)

And. I'm pregnant.

BLACKOUT

Dowager Countess So-and-So

WHERE

A sumptuous drawing room on a glorious English estate.

WHEN

The nineteen teens.

CHARACTERS

MARY – A rich young lady.

DOWAGER COUNTESS LADY EMPRESS
GRANTHAMSHANTHAMTANTAMINGHAMSHIRE –
      Her distinguished grandmother, hereafter known in the script as
      DCLEG (Think: Maggie Smith).

LORD GRANTHAMSHANTHAMTANTAMINGHAMSHIRE –
      DCLEG's son, Mary's father.

RUFUS – A butler.

MAUREEN – A scullery maid.

GARDENER – A gardener.

A NOTE ON THE TEXT

Let the saying of the Dowager's name be a feast. An increasingly impossible to say feast.

Mary and her grandmother sit in a drawing room. Rufus, their butler, lays out sandwiches and a tea service as they talk.

MARY: So, the question is: do I love him? Can I love him? Should I love him? What do you think, Grandmother?

DCLEG: Now, now, Mary. You must address me how I'm supposed to be addressed.

MARY: Sorry. Should I love him, Dowager Countess Lady Empress GranthamShanthamTantaminghamshire?

DCLEG: Oh, I don't know, Mary. Why don't—

(Rufus clangs a cup ever so slightly.)

MARY: RUFUS! You mustn't interrupt the Dowager Countess Lady Empress GranthamShanthamTantaminghamshire!

RUFUS: Sorry, ma'am.

MARY: Now, where was I?

DCLEG: Were we talking about tea?

MARY: No, that's what we're drinking.

(Lord GranthamShanthamTantaminghamshire enters with mail.)

LORD: Mum, this came for you in the mail.

(DCLEG gasps and drops whatever she's holding: the scandal!)

MARY: FATHER! Have you been trampled by a horse?

LORD: No?

MARY: Then what has gotten into you? Don't you know who you're talking to?

LORD Oh! Silly boy! How do I always forget? There's some mail for you, Dowager Countess Lady Empress GranthamShanthamTantaminghamshire.

DCLEG: I do like mail. Now, what were we talking about?

MARY: The war?

LORD: Oh, I do love talking about the war.

DCLEG: I don't think it was the war.

(Maureen, a scullery maid, appears from nowhere.)

MAUREEN: Sorry to interrupt. I've been in the corner scullerizing in silence this whole time. You were talking about Lord Arthur, friends.

(DCLEG drops everything and slides off her chair. She convulses on the floor.)

LORD: We are not your friends!

MARY: My grandfather, Count GranthamShantham, did not wed my grandmother, Lady Tantaminghamshire so that we could be your friends!

LORD: Nor did his parents, Sir Grantham and Empress Shantham!

MARY: Nor did hers, Lord Tantam and The Widow Inghamshire!

LORD: Indeed, they all must be turning over in their heavily engraved coffins!

MAUREEN: My apologies, I've completely misread the room. It won't happen again, Dowager Countess Lady Empress GranthamShanthamTantam—?

MARY: Inghamshire.

MAUREEN: Right.

DCLEG: Now, what we were talking about?

(Gardner enters.)

GARDENER: I found this necklace in the garden. Is it yours, Dowager Empress...?

(He finds himself unable to remember the rest of her name.)

Oh, golly I've lost it.

(DCLEG, Mary, and Lord drop everything and lose the ability to stand up straight.)

LORD: What is this insolence?!

MARY: This is the Dowager Countess Lady Empress GranthamShanthamTantaminghamshire's house, and in the Dowager Countess Lady Empress GranthamShanthamTantaminghamshire's house, we abide by the Dowager Countess Lady Empress GranthamShanthamTantaminghamshire's rules. Why? Because she is the Dowager Countess Lady Empress GranthamShanthamTantaminghamshire. Is that—sorry, my mouth has gone numb. Is that understood?

DCLEG: *(Still on the floor, re: a piece of mail)* Hold that thought, Mary. I've just been given a new title: Duchess. Who'd like to do the honors and christen it?

(Pandemonium as everyone scatters, leaving Mary somehow alone in the room and perhaps hiding herself behind a pillow or under a chair.)

Ah, Mary. Dear, why is your mouth quivering?

MARY: I think just general exhaustion.

DCLEG: Yes, it is exhausting being us. Now then: ready when you are.

(Mary nervously takes a huge breath and is about to speak, when:)

Actually, you know what? You can just call me "Ma'am."

MARY: Really?

DCLEG: I have always been secretly progressive, Mary. Change must be embraced.

(Small pause.)

Actually, change be damned. Say my fancy name. Say my fancy name now.

BLACKOUT

Hüntzel and Grüntzel

WHERE
A gingerbread house at the edge of a forest.

WHEN
This afternoon.

CHARACTERS
HÜNTZEL – A sweet, fragile fairytale boy in lederhosen.
GRÜTZEL – A sweet, fragile fairytale girl in lederhosen.
THE WITCH – Just a hungry, increasingly frustrated lady.

A NOTE ON THE TEXT
Hüntzel and Grützel should speak like the sort of people you'd imagine to pronounce an "ü" even if it doesn't make sense in certain words. They probably don't have to have a regionally specific accent, just something that sounds a bit Alpine or even like they're related to the Swedish Chef from *The Muppets*.

A witch puts finishing touches on her gingerbread house.

WITCH: A little poisoned frosting. Some poisoned gum drops. And the cherry on top is a poisoned cherry…on top!

(She finds herself hilarious and does a gloriously witchy laugh.)

I smell children!

(Hüntzel and Grützel enter. Grützel drops breadcrumbs behind them.)

GRÜTZEL: Oh Hüntzel, lük! A gingerbrüd hüs!

HÜNTZEL: Oh wü, Grützel! Wü!

BOTH: Yümmy!

WITCH: Hello, sweet children. You lost?

HÜNTZEL: Lost and hüngry.

GRÜTZEL: I am hüngry tü.

BOTH: *(Perhaps a touch too intense)* We are büth so hüngry.

WITCH: Hunger. Yes, I can empathize. Here. Have some gingerbread.

(She breaks off a piece of the house and offers it to them.)

Definitely not poisoned. Enjoy!

GRÜTZEL: Oh wü!   HÜNTZEL: Yümmy yüm!

GRÜTZEL (CON'T): Büt lük clüsely, Hüntzel! I have a bad feeling about this gingerbrüd. It may be füll…of glüten.

HÜNTZEL: Wü, good catch, Grützel! We'd better nüt eat them. I am a nice boy except after ze glüten.

GRÜTZEL: Then he is stück on the toilet jüst flüshin'.

WITCH: Thank you for that detail. No problem. I have plenty of gluten free treats. Lollipop? Also not poisoned.

(She pulls out two giant lollipops. The kids instantly stop panicking.)

GRÜTZEL: Amüzing!   HÜNTZEL: Delücious!

HÜNTZEL (CON'T): Büt, üh nü! Are they prüssessed?

WITCH: What is "prüssessed?"

GRÜTZEL: Yü knü. When you prüssess sümething.

WITCH: You mean, "processed?""

GRÜTZEL: *(An affirmative)* Üh-hüh.

WITCH: I mean, it's candy. So, probably yeah?

HÜNTZEL: Büt ür büdies are spücial!

GRÜTZEL: We're spücial people!

HÜNTZEL: What is wrüng with yü, lüdy?!

GRÜTZEL: You münster!

WITCH: I'm actually a witch.

GRÜTZEL: Let's gü, Hüntzel! This münster doesn't respect our büdies.

WITCH: *(Offended)* Now, hang on a second. What about you? Isn't there gluten in the breadcrumbs you're dropping?

GRÜTZEL: Üh nü! I didn't realize!

HÜNTZEL: Oh nü, Grützel!

GRÜTZEL: Why Güd?! It bürns!

WITCH: Is the bread actually hurting you?

GRÜTZEL: The pain is emütional!

HÜNTZEL: EMÜTIONAL!

BOTH: WE ARE BÜTH SO HÜNGRY

HÜNTZEL: ÜRGH!

GRÜTZEL: ÜRGH!

(They start to leave.)

WITCH: Ok, uh, wow. Wait, sweet, special—I mean, "spücial" children. I can see I have misstepped. I'm sorry my snack choices have offended. Could I make it up to you with…a not-poisoned apple?

(She pulls out two apples.)

HÜNTZEL: Ür they üthically sürced?

WITCH: Ethically sourced? Don't know. But this is: from my garden—a not-poisoned tomato?

GRÜTZEL: Is it heirlüm?

WITCH: Ok, how 'bout a not-poisoned steak?

GRÜTZEL: Wüs üt hüppy whün üt wüs alüve?

WITCH: Forget food. Poison-free ice water?

GRÜTZEL: My güms are sensitive.

WITCH: Poison-free plain water.

HÜNTZEL From a single üse büttle?!

WITCH: Plain tap water.

GRÜTZEL: Flüoride rüins ür münd.

WITCH: Whatever. Just come inside, check out my oven. Grab a chair.

HÜNTZEL: Is the matürial reüsed?

WITCH: Or stand by the window.

HÜNTZEL: But whüt if I fül?

WITCH: We'll close the window.

GRÜTZEL: Büt whüt üf I lük thrü üt ünd smüsh my hüd ün the glüs?

WITCH: You know what? I give up!

HÜNTZEL: You mean, "üp."

WITCH: Whatever. I'm just an old witch lady who's hungry.

GRÜTZEL: We're hüngry tü!   HÜNTZEL: We are so hüngry!
　ÜRGH!　　　　　　　　　ÜRGH!

WITCH: Well, what can you even eat?! Me?!

(The kids perk up.)

HÜNTZEL: Now thüt's an idea.   GRÜTZEL: Yümmy yüm.

(They begin to advance.)

WITCH: *(Desperate)* Now wait. You can't eat me! I've eaten bread! And processed food!

(They pull out all sorts of "cheat" food items: ketchup, whipped cream, a big saltshaker, butter. Also forks and knives. Big knives.)

HÜNTZEL: Can yü keep a secrüt?

BOTH: So hüve we.

(They pounce on the witch and begin to eat her.)

BLACKOUT

One Upping Your Ex

WHERE

A city street.

WHEN

This afternoon.

CHARACTERS

JEFF
TONY

Jeff and Tony bump into each other in the street.

JEFF: Hello, ex-boyfriend!
TONY: Wow. Hi.

(They share an awkward hug.)

JEFF: How are you?
TONY: Good. I'm good. Still in—?
JEFF: Yup. Same apartment, same roommate. You?
TONY: I got a house.
JEFF: Cool.
TONY: Yeah. Cool. Alright, I should probably [go]—
JEFF: You look good.
TONY: Thanks. I finally got into shape.
JEFF: It really suits you.
TONY: Thanks.
JEFF: You can't tell through these clothes, but I got into shape too. Well, a
    shape. My body is a different shape than it was before.
TONY: I see that.
JEFF: Thank you. I know. And it no longer creaks, which is...win!

(Leaving)

Anyway, nice to—
TONY: I got a new job!
JEFF: Congrats!
TONY: Thanks! I'm a partner at a law firm.
JEFF: Amazing. Wait. We broke up, like, a year ago. When did you go to
    law school?
TONY: I went online. And then I aggressively stepped on a bunch of
    people's necks and forged some documents that may or may not be
    the reason those people arc now in jail. So, yeah. I'm a partner.
    You still a struggling actor?
JEFF: No.
TONY: *(Delighting in this)* You gave up your dreams. Such a shame.

(Leaving)

Bye!

JEFF: No, I quit because I started my own business.

TONY: Oh, congrats!

JEFF: Yeah, it's a marketing company. It's multi-level. It's a multi-level marketing company. We sell leggings that are intense emotions in color form.

TONY: Wow.

JEFF: Thank you. I know. And! Nobody thinks it's a scam because it's not a scam, so yeah, I'm doing very well financially.

TONY: Congrats! So am I.

JEFF: Congrats! Ok, bye!

TONY: I'm not finished. Yeah, I mean my job pays me so much money— like so much—but there's another reason why I'm enviably rich. I met someone.

JEFF: ...Oh?

TONY: Yeah. A rich someone. You seeing anyone?

JEFF: No, I'm. I'm still.

TONY: Alone?

JEFF: Yeah.

TONY: Well, I met an incredible man named Elmer. I'll admit it was kind of hard at first, because he was a lot older than most of the guys I'd been with. He was 99 when we met. It felt like a sign, because 99th was the percentile I was in at my online law school.

JEFF: Wow.

TONY: Anyway, Elmer loved books and talking about life during the Great Depression. He had a great sense of humor. Always joking about things like heart attacks, seizures. So funny. But then he had an actual heart attack. I thought he was kidding, and was laughing until I wasn't, because he died in front of me. But! He left me a ton of money and a house, so I'll never have to work again. I'm so happy. Bye!

JEFF: I'm so happy too. I've stopped screaming into the mirror, "Why is this my life? Why is this my life?"

TONY: Same! I'm so confidant since I got in shape!

JEFF: Yeah! It's great being in this shape that doesn't creak.

TONY: Ok, bye!

JEFF: Bye!

TONY: Bye!
JEFF: I'm going now!
TONY: I am too!

(They each start to leave, but suddenly they turn and run to each other. They passionately kiss/eat each other's mouths.)

Oh God, I've missed you!
JEFF: I missed you too!

(They feel each other's bodies.)

I think you were lying about your body.

(Jeff's body begins to creak.)

TONY: So were you!

BLACKOUT

Colin Waitt is a playwright, producer and performer. His plays have been produced by The Tank, The Peoples Improv Theater, This Is Not a Theater Company, Dixon Place and Barn Arts. He has been a member of various writing groups, including Art House Productions's INKubator, The Pilot Program at The Tank and an informal group that's met weekly since 2016 but never figured out what to call itself. He was a finalist for Red Bull Theater's Short New Play Festival, Davenport Theatricals's 10 Minute Play Contest and The Project Y Writer's Group. His play, *Fair*, was a semifinalist for the National Playwrights Conference at the Eugene O'Neill Theater Center.

Colin produced the original sell-out run of *Puffs, or: Seven Increasingly Eventful Years at a Certain School of Magic and Magic* at The Peoples Improv Theater. He was an Associate Producer on its record-breaking Off-Broadway run. Additional producing highlights include *SERIALS* at The Flea Theater, *Kapow-i GoGo* at The Peoples Improv Theater and associate producing *Our House in Concert* in London's West End.

Memorable acting credits include playing Jesus in the Drama Desk Award-winning production of *The Mysteries* at The Flea Theater, performing *Pool Play* in an actual pool at The International Theatre Festival of Kerala in India with This Is Not a Theater Company and originating the role of General President Thunderbolt in *Kapow-i GoGo*. Colin trained formally as an actor at The Royal Central School of Speech and Drama, having previously earned his B.A. in Theater Studies from The University of Minnesota—Twin Cities.

Made in the USA
Monee, IL
04 May 2024

57953344R00167